The Best of
SEWING MACHINE
Fun FOR kids

second edition

Ready? Set... SEW!

PROJECTS & 37 ACTIVITIES

LYNDA MILLIGAN & NANCY SMITH

FunStitch
S T U D I O
an imprint of C&T Publishing

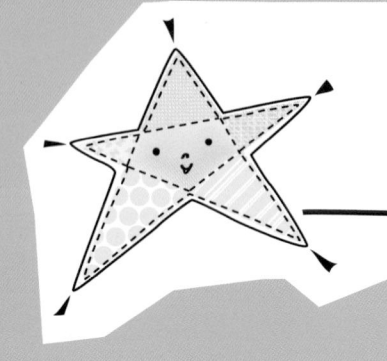

THIS BOOK BELONGS TO:

_____

Text copyright © 2016 by Lynda Milligan and Nancy Smith

Photography and artwork copyright © 2016 by C&T Publishing, Inc.

PUBLISHER: Amy Marson

CREATIVE DIRECTOR: Gailen Runge

EDITOR: Lynn Koolish

TECHNICAL EDITOR: Debbie Rodgers

COVER/BOOK DESIGNER / ILLUSTRATOR: Kerry Graham

PRODUCTION COORDINATOR: Zinnia Heinzmann

PRODUCTION EDITORS: Jessica Brotman and Jennifer Warren

Photography by Diane Pedersen, unless otherwise noted

Published by FunStitch Studio, an imprint of C&T Publishing, Inc., P.O. Box 1456, Lafayette, CA 94549

Attention Teachers: C&T Publishing, Inc., encourages you to use this book as a text for teaching. Contact us at 800-284-1114 or ctpub.com for lesson plans and information about the C&T Creative Troupe.

Library of Congress Cataloging-in-Publication Data

Names: Milligan, Lynda, 1951- author. | Smith, Nancy, 1943 October 17- author.

Title: The best of sewing machine fun for kids : ready, set, sew - 37 projects & activities / Lynda Milligan and Nancy Smith.

Description: 2nd edition. | Lafayette, CA : FunStitch Studio, an imprint of C&T Publishing, Inc., [2016] | Audience: Ages 7+_

Identifiers: LCCN 2015044811 | ISBN 9781617452635 (soft cover)

Subjects: LCSH: Machine sewing--Juvenile literature. | Handicraft--Juvenile literature. | Sewing--Juvenile literature.

Classification: LCC SF395.5 .G56 2016 | DDC 646.2--dc23

LC record available at http://lccn.loc.gov/2015044811

Printed in Malaysia

10 9 8 7 6

CONTENTS

PROJECTS

"I'M BORED. WHAT CAN I DO?"

Don't panic. This is a book just for you, packed with exciting sewing adventures that you will love. Explore all the fun of learning a new craft and trying new materials. Then experiment on your own.

Be sure to play the games and work the puzzles as you go. Besides being fun, they will help you to remember important information.

Work page by page through the book, discovering new skills with each project.

Ask your Helper Star when you don't know what to do next. A Helper Star is anyone who knows more about sewing than you do. It may be your mother or father, your grandparent, an older brother or sister, or even a friend.

You are ready to begin. Enjoy your first adventure into the world of sewing. You can teach yourself!

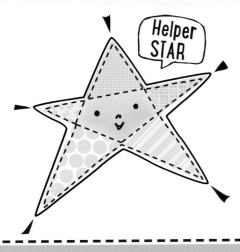

Helper STAR

A NOTE TO HELPER STARS

The Helper Star's job is to be available for extra help. The younger the beginning sewist, the more help he or she will need. A Helper Star is anyone who knows more about sewing than the new sewist. One area where you can help is winding and inserting the bobbin, as this procedure varies from machine to machine. Be sure to have the sewing machine manual for easy reference.

ABOUT THIS BOOK

The "I'm bored, what can I do?" syndrome can strike fear in the hearts of parents. Don't despair! Don't panic! You're holding the answer in your hands. *The Best of Sewing Machine Fun for Kids* will jump-start the creativity in any child. It is packed with exciting games and activities that kids will love to do. Our panel of experts (kids ages 7–17) suggested, tested, and approved each and every one.

The goal of each activity is to have a successful skill-building experience and to develop sewing self-confidence. Materials needed are inexpensive and easy to find around the house or wherever sewing, fabric, or craft supplies are sold.

There are puzzle pages and patterns in this book that are meant to be traced. If you prefer, you can download and print them at **http://tinyurl.com/11173-patterns-download**.

We recommend that children learn to sew on a full-size sewing machine that is in good repair. A child is ready when he or she has enough coordination to handle scissors, small pins and needles, and can sit comfortably at the machine with feet flat on the floor. If the child is not tall enough at a regular table, find a shorter table or raise the foot pedal. The new sewist should also be responsible enough to know about the safe use of the iron and sewing machine. See Safety First! (page 7) before starting.

The Best of Sewing Machine Fun for Kids and a little encouragement will open the door to a lifetime of creative adventure. **Creative kids are happy kids!** ☺

LET'S GO!

Find these seven parts on your sewing machine. Once you have found them, you are ready to start your journey into the creative land of sewing.

A Thread Take-Up

Stop and start with this lever in its highest position to keep your needle from unthreading.

B Presser Foot Lifter

It is usually located on the back of the machine. Use it to raise and lower the presser foot. Raise it to insert or remove fabric. Lower it when ready to sew.

C Presser Foot

When lowered, it surrounds the needle and holds the fabric in place while you sew.

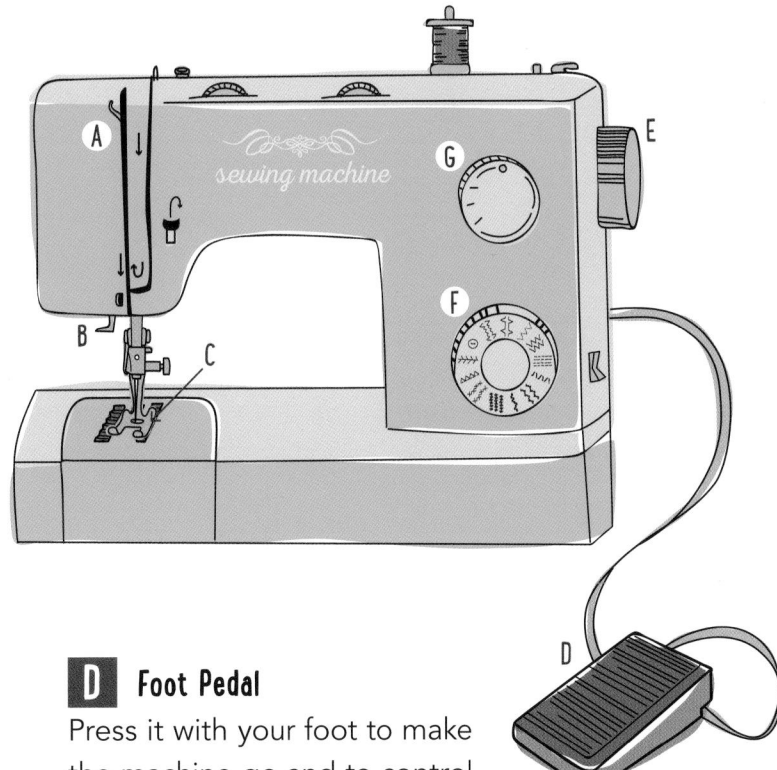

D Foot Pedal

Press it with your foot to make the machine go and to control speed. Raise your foot to stop.

E Flywheel

The flywheel, located on the right-hand side of the machine, turns as the machine goes. By turning the flywheel toward yourself, you can raise and lower the needle to place it exactly where you want it.

F Stitch Width Selector

Adjust this dial or lever on the front of the machine to change a straight stitch to a zigzag stitch. Use a straight stitch for the projects in this book unless told otherwise.

G Stitch Length Selector

This changes the length of your stitch. All activities in this book use a medium-length stitch, which is halfway between the smallest number and the largest number. Adjust the dial or lever for this stitch length now.

SAFETY FIRST!

Find ten unsafe things in this picture. To download and print this page, refer to About This Book (page 5).

To check your answers, see Puzzle Answers (page 124).

DISCOVER STITCHING

Experiment by stitching without thread on notebook paper lines. Learn to control the speed and smoothness with a little practice.

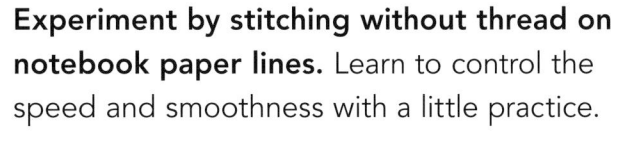

1. Remove all the thread from your machine. Plug it in and turn it on.

2. Raise the presser foot by raising the presser foot lifter. Put a piece of notebook paper under the presser foot. Lower the needle onto a line by turning the flywheel toward you. Turn the paper so you will be able to stitch along the line.

3. Lower the presser foot by lowering the presser foot lifter.

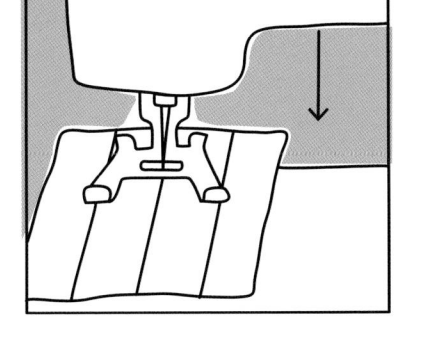

1. Turn the flywheel toward you and gently step on the foot pedal to start the machine.

2. As your machine begins to stitch along the line, take your hand off the flywheel. Lightly guide the paper by making a triangle with your hands to frame the stitching area. Let the machine take the paper. Do not pull or push—just guide.

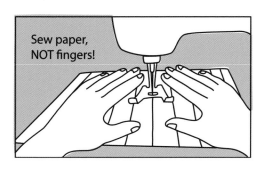

Sew paper, NOT fingers!

3. To stop the machine, take your foot off the pedal. Turn the flywheel by hand until the thread take-up is in the highest position.

4. Raise the presser foot and move the paper over to the next line. Lower the presser foot.

5. Practice starting, stopping, and guiding the paper. After finishing each row, check to see that the needle has punched holes along the line. Stitch along several lines until you feel comfortable.

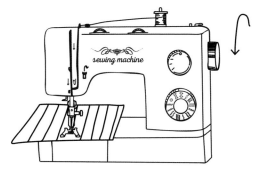

Helper Star Hint

Introduce the sewing machine manual to your beginning stitcher to help him or her find the speed control. Some machines have a half-speed control which can be helpful. If your machine does not have this control but has a foot pedal that is hinged. try inserting a new. soft sponge into the hinge to slow down the speed and give your stitcher more control.

MOUSE PIVOTS

Stitch a path for the mouse to find the cheese.

 □ pencil

□ copy paper

 Place copy paper over the rectangle below and trace, or download and print the page. (Refer to About This Book, page 5.)

1. Place the paper with the design under the presser foot. Lower the needle into position at the mouse. Stitch on the line. Stop at the first corner.

2. To pivot: Leave the needle down in the paper. If the needle is up, turn the flywheel by hand to put the needle down. Lift the presser foot. Swing the paper around and lower the presser foot. What an awesome pivot!

To Pivot

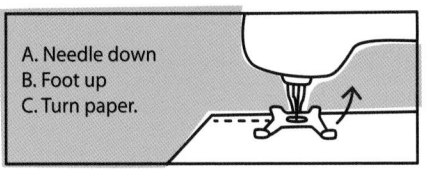

A. Needle down
B. Foot up
C. Turn paper.

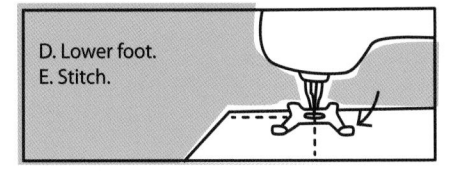

D. Lower foot.
E. Stitch.

3. Stitch to the next corner. Pivot again.

4. Play, practice, and enjoy stitching on the lines. Raise the presser foot to remove the paper. Is your thread take-up at the highest position? Did your mouse find the cheese?

Helper Star Hint

Instead of tracing designs, make copies on a copy machine.

What do you do when a mouse squeaks?

HA! HA! HA!

Oil it!

11

YOUR MACHINE

Nineteen incredible parts to know!

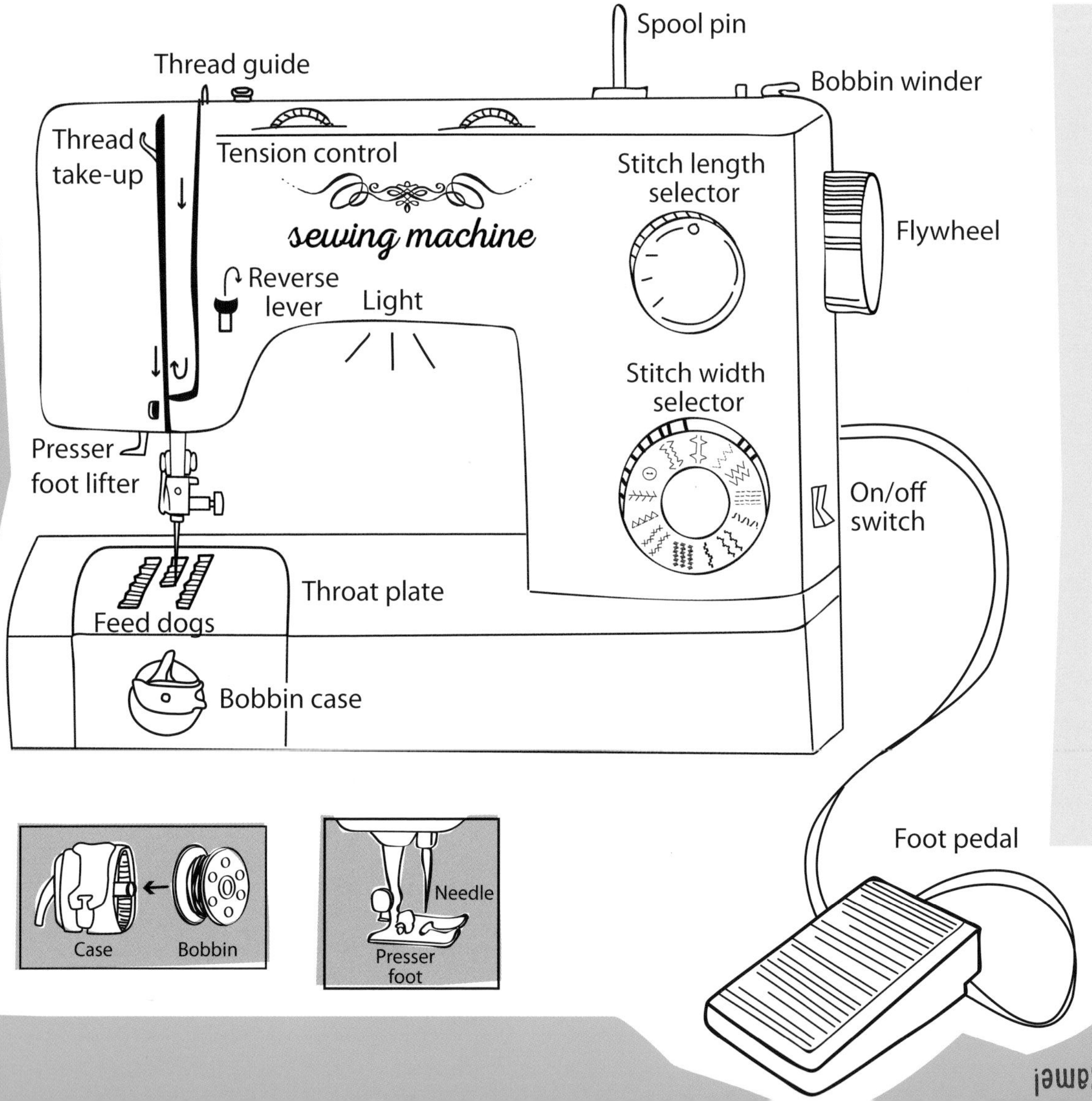

☞ Knock, knock. Who's there? Lettuce. Lettuce who?

Spool pin

Thread guide

Bobbin winder

Thread take-up

Tension control

sewing machine

Stitch length selector

Flywheel

Reverse lever

Light

Stitch width selector

On/off switch

Presser foot lifter

Throat plate

Feed dogs

Bobbin case

Case   Bobbin

Needle

Presser foot

Foot pedal

Sewing Machine Manual

Helper Star Hint

The parts defined and illustrated on these two pages are on all sewing machines. Check your sewing machine manual to find the exact location of each of these parts on your machine.

HA! HA! HA!

Lettuce play another game!

Bobbin Case and Bobbin

The bobbin case holds the bobbin, and the bobbin holds the bottom thread. How fast can you say "Betty brought bright brass bobbins"?

Bobbin Winder

The winder holds the bobbin when the thread is wound from the spool to the bobbin.

Feed Dogs

The feed dogs' teeth and presser foot work together to move the fabric under the needle. Look closely to see the teeth!

Flywheel

The flywheel turns as the machine goes. By turning the flywheel toward yourself, you can raise and lower the needle to place it exactly where you want it. When you stop or start, turn the flywheel until the thread take-up is in its highest position.

Foot Pedal

Press the pedal with your foot to make the machine go and to control speed. Raise your foot to stop.

Light

It shines on the sewing area so you can see better.

Needle

The needle carries the thread through the fabric, where it joins with the bobbin thread to create a stitch.

On/Off Switch

The switch turns the power on and off.

Presser Foot

The presser foot and the feed dogs work together to move the fabric under the needle. Presser feet are available with different shapes for different purposes. An all-purpose foot is used for the activities in this book.

Presser Foot Lifter

Use the lifter to raise and lower the presser foot. Raise it to insert or remove the fabric. Lower it when ready to sew.

Reverse Lever or Button

Use the reverse lever or button to sew backwards.

Spool Pin

This spindle holds the spool of thread in place.

Stitch Length Selector

Adjust the dial or lever to set the length of the stitch.

Stitch Width Selector

Adjust the dial or lever to change a straight stitch to a zigzag stitch.

Tension Control

This dial controls the amount of pressure on the thread as it passes through the machine. It usually does not need to be adjusted. Refer to your machine manual.

Thread Guides

The guides direct the thread from the spool to the needle.

Thread Take-Up

This lever helps to keep tension on the thread. By turning the flywheel by hand, you can stop and start with the lever in its highest position. This will prevent your needle from unthreading.

Throat Plate

This metal plate has openings for the needle and the feed dogs.

PATTI'S PUZZLE

Trace this maze onto a piece of copy paper or download and print the page. (Refer to About This Book, page 5.) **Stitch between the lines instead of on the lines.** How many perfect pivots can you make?

Practical Patti Potter patiently placed perfect pivots upon pieces of pretty pink paper.

To check your answer, see Puzzle Answers (page 124).

If all the cars in the country were pink, what would we have?

HA! HA! HA!

A pink car nation!

CLIMB THE PEAKS AND RIDE THE WAVES

1. Trace the lines on this page onto a piece of copy paper or download and print the page. (Refer to About This Book, page 5.) Stitch along the mountain peaks. **Try to keep the mountain climber from falling off the trail.** Keep your peaks nice and sharp by perfecting those pivots.

2. Stitch along the ocean waves.
Try to keep your surfer from wiping out.

3. For extra fun, draw your own creative lines to stitch.

☞ What's the difference between a hill and a pill?

Slow down for curves.

Ones hard to get up. Ones hard to get down.

HA! HA! HA!

15

PLACE THE PARTS

Draw a line from the name of each part to its correct location. To download and print the page, refer to About This Book (page 5). Check your answers by looking at the sewing machine diagram (Your Machine, page 12).

Thread guide

Thread take-up

Presser foot lifter

Reverse lever

Feed dogs

Throat plate

Bobbin case

Light

Tension control

Stitch length selector

Spool pin

Bobbin winder

Flywheel

On/off switch

Foot pedal

Stitch width selector

Needle

Presser foot

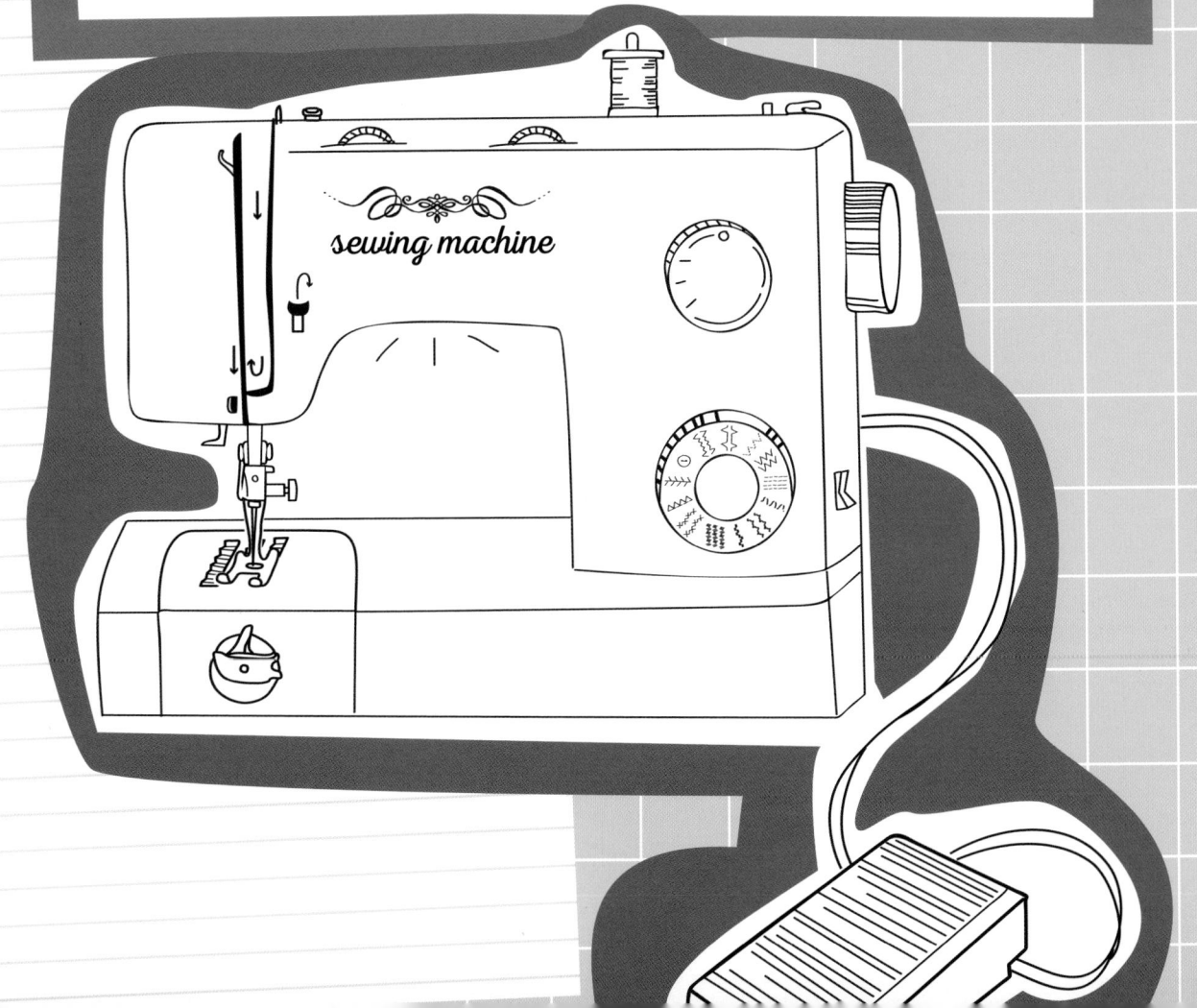

sewing machine

STITCH ALONG

Can you stitch these shapes without lifting the needle from the paper and without double-stitching any line? Remember that there may be more than one answer. Trace the designs on copy paper, copy the page on a copier, or download and print the page. (Refer to About This Book, page 5.) To check your answers, see Puzzle Answers (page 124).

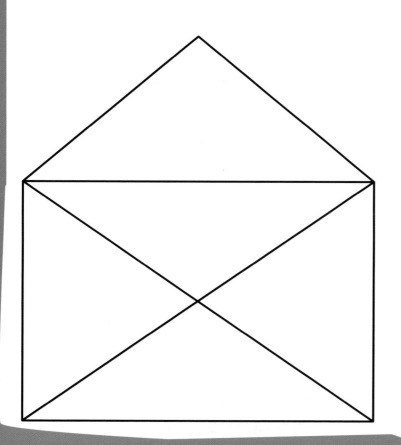

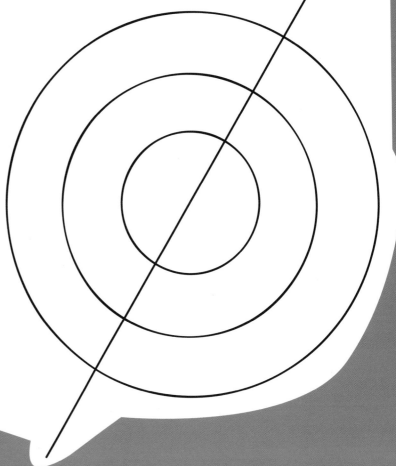

TANGLED THREADS

Draw a line from each scrambled word in the first column to the solution in the second column. To download and print this page, refer to About This Book (page 5).

serveer reevl ro nottub	spool pin
sseerrp toof	thread guide
thicst gelnth sorteecl	tension control
bibbon	needle
helewylf	reverse lever or button
no/fof chwits	feed dogs
cishtt thwid loreects	presser foot
loosp nip	thread take-up
defe odsg	presser foot lifter
rohtta tepla	flywheel
nestnio troncol	foot pedal
leeend	stitch length selector
dareth degiu	stitch width selector
otof dalep	light
dareth kate-pu	bobbin
nobbib drwine	bobbin winder
serpers ooft terfil	throat plate
gitlh	on/off switch

Find the following words hidden in the puzzle below. They may be backward or upside down!

stitch	tension	sew
needle	scissors	bobbin
pins	light	flywheel
feed dogs	plug	rip

M	F	L	Y	W	H	E	E	L	G
W	E	S	T	P	K	P	W	S	Y
D	E	Q	X	I	Z	J	B	K	E
V	D	T	E	N	S	I	O	N	L
P	D	H	H	S	T	C	B	M	D
I	O	G	P	R	I	G	B	K	E
R	G	I	L	N	T	V	I	C	E
Q	S	L	U	B	C	F	N	D	N
H	M	T	G	L	H	J	W	X	W
S	R	O	S	S	I	C	S	T	Q

To check your answers, see Puzzle Answers (page 124).

SEEK AND SPELL

How many words can you make from the words SEWING MACHINE?

We found more than 165. Remember plurals! To download and print the page, refer to About This Book (page 5).

YOUR SCORE?

140+	Eagle Eyes
100-139	Looking Good
60-99	I Spy More Words
20-59	Keep Looking

To check your answers, see Puzzle Answers (page 124).

S
N
A
W
E
I
G
C
M
H
E

THREAD THE MACHINE

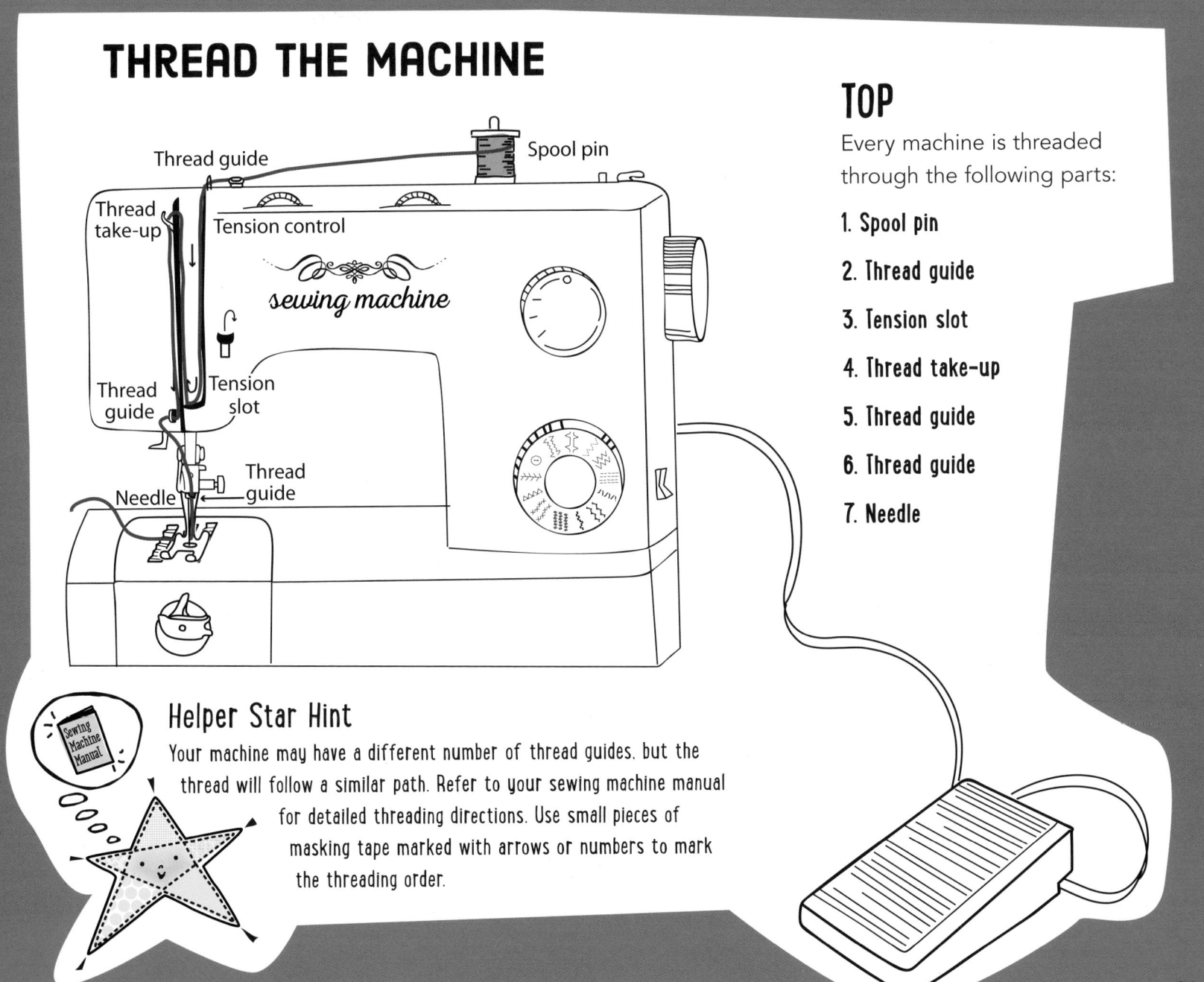

Thread guide

Spool pin

Thread take-up

Tension control

sewing machine

Thread guide

Tension slot

Needle

Thread guide

TOP

Every machine is threaded through the following parts:

1. **Spool pin**

2. **Thread guide**

3. **Tension slot**

4. **Thread take-up**

5. **Thread guide**

6. **Thread guide**

7. **Needle**

Helper Star Hint

Sewing Machine Manual

Your machine may have a different number of thread guides, but the thread will follow a similar path. Refer to your sewing machine manual for detailed threading directions. Use small pieces of masking tape marked with arrows or numbers to mark the threading order.

Needle

The needle is round on the front and flat on the back so that it cannot be inserted backwards. On the round side of the needle is a groove. Find the groove by running your fingernail down the needle. When the needle is in the machine correctly, the thread will travel down the groove and through the eye. Put the needle in your machine. Thread the machine. Does the thread travel down the groove and through the eye of the needle?

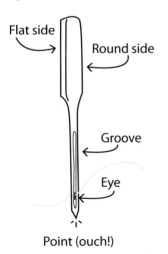

Flat side
Round side
Groove
Eye
Point (ouch!)

Winding the Bobbin and Inserting the Bobbin Case

Because machines are different, check your sewing machine manual to see how to wind your bobbin and how to thread your bobbin case. Pay strict attention to the direction the thread comes off the bobbin and the way the bobbin is put into the bobbin case.

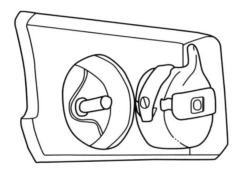

Pulling Up the Bobbin Thread

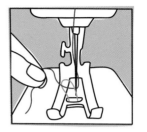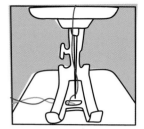

After threading the needle, pull the thread out to the left side under the presser foot. Hold the thread while turning the flywheel toward yourself one full turn. Tug gently and the thread will pull up a loop of the bobbin thread. Pull both threads under the presser foot and toward the back of the machine.

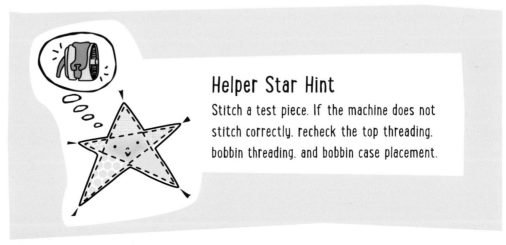

Helper Star Hint

Stitch a test piece. If the machine does not stitch correctly, recheck the top threading, bobbin threading, and bobbin case placement.

BUILDING BLOCKS

These machine parts are important to know before you can create with confidence. To download and print this page, refer to About This Book (page 5).

1. The _____ _____ _____ lifts and lowers the presser foot. Raise it to insert or remove fabric. Lower it when ready to sew.

2. The _____ _____ _____ adjusts the length of the stitch.

3. The _____ _____ _____ changes a straight stitch to a zigzag stitch.

4. Turn the _____ to raise and lower the needle to place it where you want it.

5. The _____ adjusts the amount of pressure on the thread as it goes through the machine.

6. The _____ and the presser foot work together to move the fabric.

7. The _____ _____ turns the power on and off.

8. Press the _____ _____ _____ _____ to sew backwards.

9. The _____ _____ directs the thread from the spool to the needle.

10. The _____ holds the bobbin thread and fits into the bobbin case.

11. Press the _____ _____ to make the sewing machine go and to control speed.

12. The _____ shines on the sewing area so you can see the needle and thread better.

13. The _____ _____ holds the bobbin when winding thread onto it.

14. The _____ _____ has openings for the needle and the feed dogs.

15. The _____ _____ holds the spool of thread in place.

16. The _____ _____ and the feed dogs work together to move the fabric.

17. The _____ _____ keeps tension on the thread. Start and stop with this lever in its highest position.

18. The _____ carries the thread through the fabric and joins it with the bobbin thread.

To check your answers, see Puzzle Answers (page 124).

SEWING BASKET

This picture shows the items you will need in your sewing basket or close to your machine. **Make a list in the space provided.** To download and print the page, refer to About This Book (page 5). Check your answers on the Puzzle Answers page (page 124) to see if your list was complete. Make sure to gather these items into your sewing basket or have them nearby when a project notes "sewing basket" in the Ready list.

DOT-TO-DOT STITCHING

Now you are ready to stitch a picture!

READY?

- ☐ pencil
- ☐ thread
- ☐ copy paper

SET?

1. Trace, photocopy, or download and print the dot-to-dots. (Refer to About This Book, page 5.)

2. Thread your sewing machine.

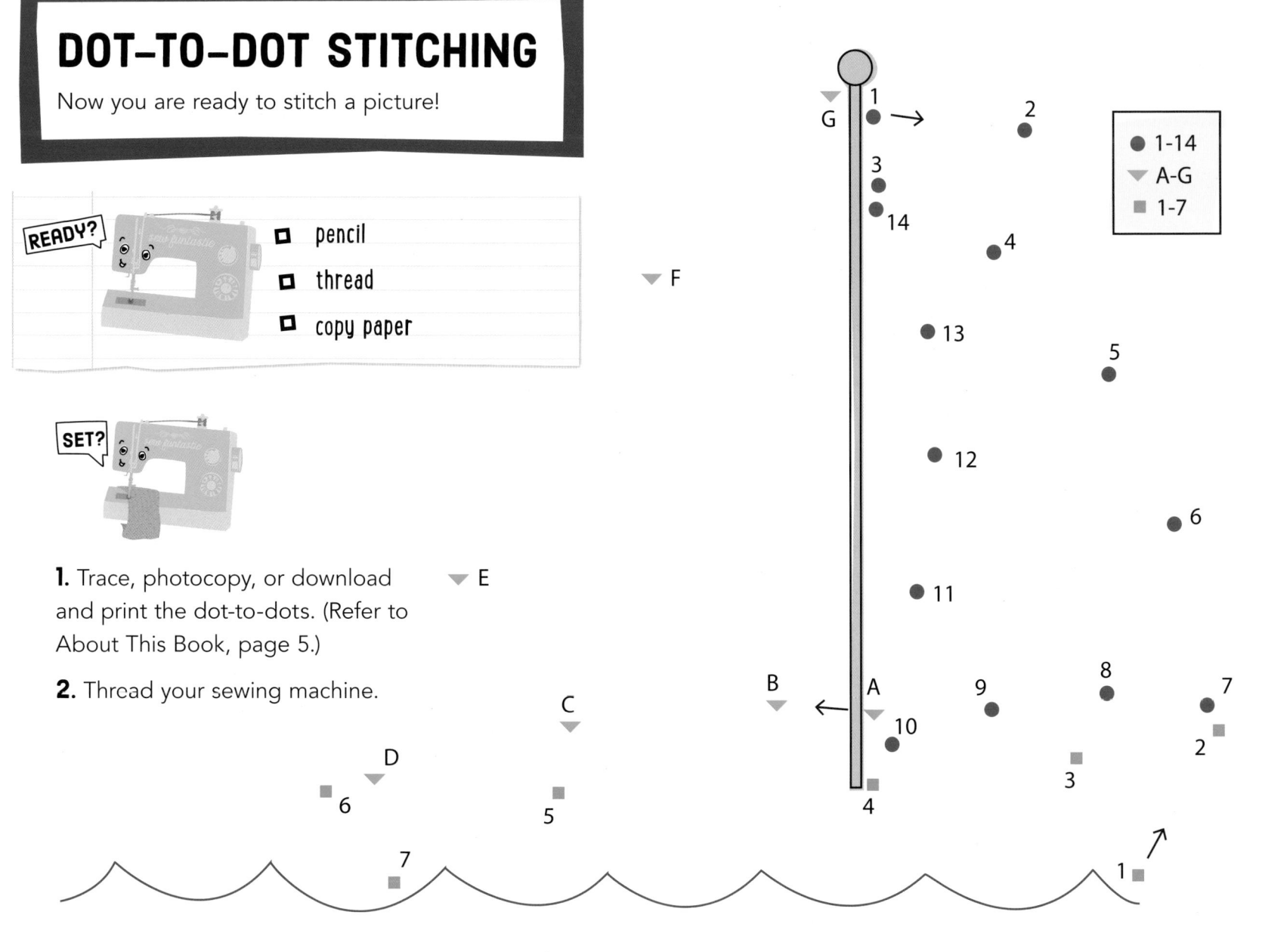

● 1-14
▼ A-G
■ 1-7

SEW!

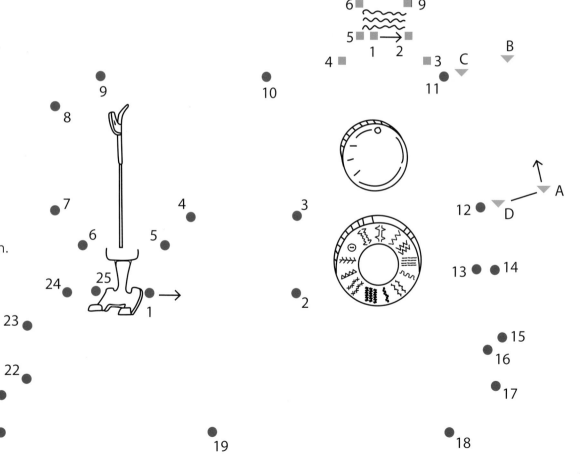

● 1-25
■ 1-9
▼ A-D

1. Start at any #1 or A symbol. Lower the needle into position at the #1 or A, ready to stitch in the direction indicated by the arrow. Lower your presser foot and begin stitching to the next number or letter of the same symbol. Stop with your needle down. Pivot if necessary. Look ahead to the next symbol instead of watching the needle. Change thread colors for different symbols. Complete the design.

7 ■   ■ 8

6 ■   ■ 9

5 ■   ■   → ■
     1   2

4 ■   ■ 3   C   B
                         ▼   ▼
                              11

9   10

8

7   4   3

6   12 ●   ▼   ▼ A
                                              D
5

24   25   13 ● ● 14
     1 →

23 ●
                                              ● 15
22 ●
21 ●   ● 16

20 ●   ● 17
        19   18

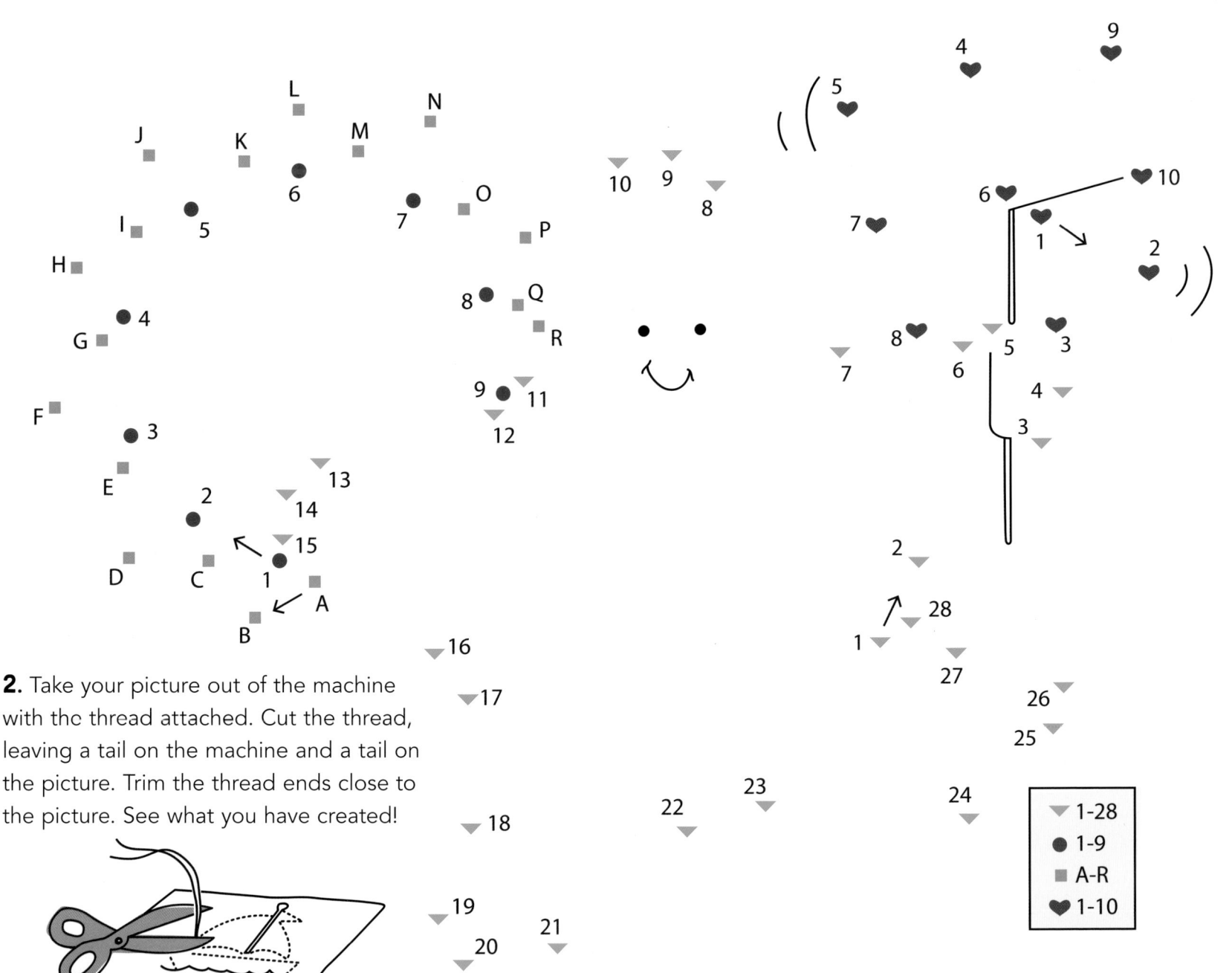

2. Take your picture out of the machine with the thread attached. Cut the thread, leaving a tail on the machine and a tail on the picture. Trim the thread ends close to the picture. See what you have created!

Dot's enough!

27

CROSSWORD PUZZLE

To download and print this page, refer to About This Book (page 5).
To check your answers, see Puzzle Answers (page 124).

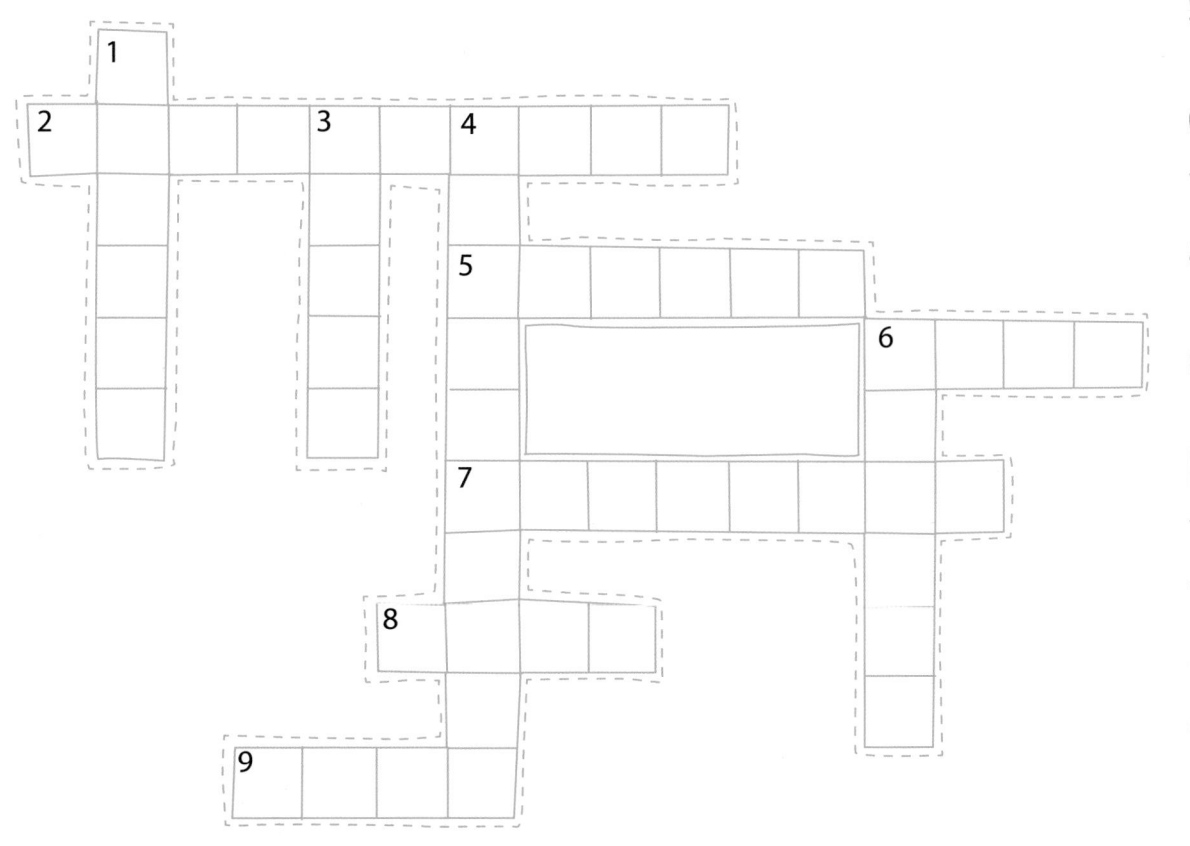

Across

2. Takes out stitches

5. Has a hole in it to hold the thread

6. _____ measure

7. Cutting tool

8. These secure fabric pieces together before sewing

9. Takes wrinkles out of fabric

Down

1. Use it for marking

3. Use it for measuring

4. A place to put pins

6. Used with a needle to stitch fabric together

PAPER–BACKED FUSIBLE WEB

Paper-backed fusible web consists of two layers—a fusible web and a paper backing. The fusible web side is bumpy and the paper backing side is smooth. It is very easy to use and is used in many projects in this book. Our favorite paper-backed fusible web is Pellon 805 Wonder-Under.

There are six steps for the process. Refer to individual project directions in the book for specific changes in these directions.

1. TRACE your shape on the paper (smooth) side.

2. CUT OUT the shape about ⅛″–¼″ away from the line unless the pattern directions tell you differently.

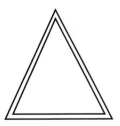

3. PRESS the fusible (bumpy) side of your shape onto the **WRONG** side of your fabric using a hot, dry iron. Press each part of the shape for about 8–10 seconds. Let it cool.

4. CUT OUT your shape on the line. Peel the paper backing away from the fabric shape.

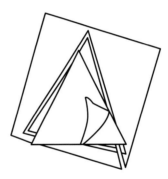

5. PLACE your fused shape on the fabric or paper background.

6. PRESS with a hot, dry iron for 8–10 seconds to fuse the shape to the background.

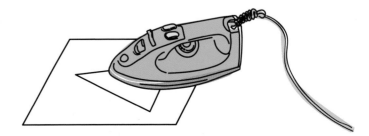

DRIVER'S TRAINING

Test your machine driving skills. Negotiate streets, alleys, and dead ends.

- ☐ thread
- ☐ copy paper
- ☐ sewing basket

READY?

Trace the design, make a copy on a copy machine, or download and print the page. (Refer to About This Book, page 5.)

SET?

SEW!

1. Begin stitching at the car.

2. Steer your way through the maze, collecting only the items you need for your sewing basket. A new item to look for is a chopstick. A chopstick is used to push out points after turning a project right side out.

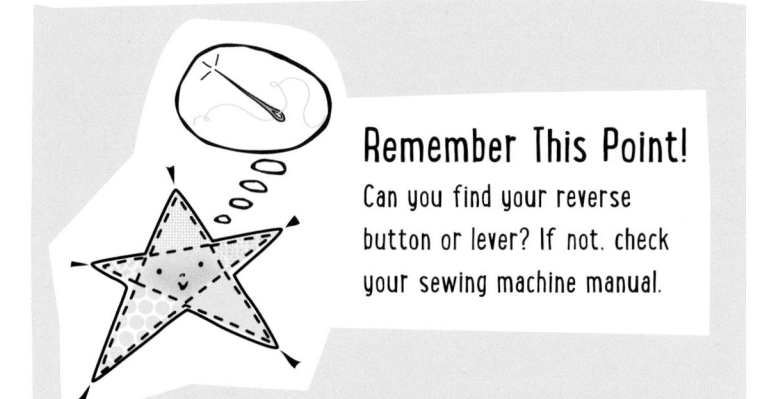

Remember This Point!
Can you find your reverse button or lever? If not, check your sewing machine manual.

3. Stitch into the item and stop.

4. Hold down the reverse button or lever and backstitch (reverse sew) to get out.

5. Continue until you have collected all nine items and found your way home.

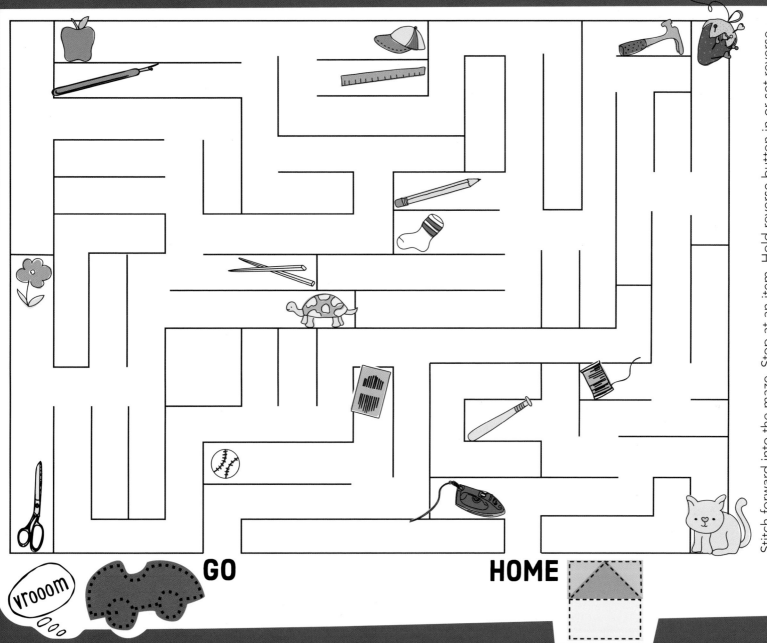

Stitch forward into the maze. Stop at an item. Hold reverse button in or set reverse lever. Backstitch. Stop. Release button or reset lever for forward stitching. Continue sewing to the next item. To check your solution, see Puzzle Answers (page 124).

GO

vrooom

HOME

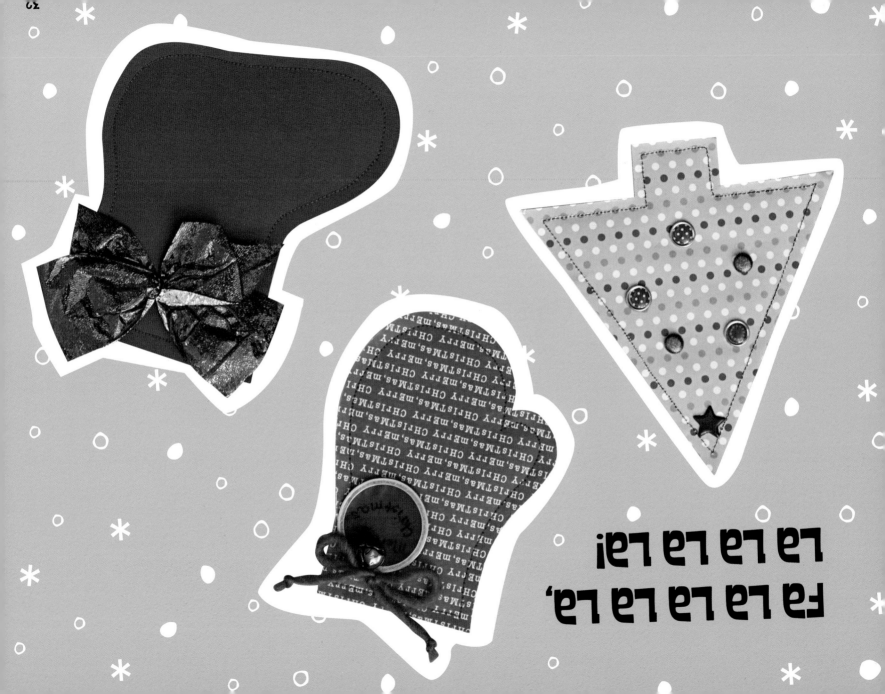

PAPER SHAPES

Making these shapes will help you feel more comfortable stitching around shapes and pivoting. You will also learn a fun technique for making patterns.

READY?

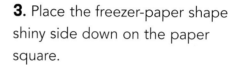

- ☐ glue
- ☐ pinking scissors (optional)
- ☐ sewing basket (page 23)

- ☐ **paper towel:** *6″ × 6″* (16 cm × 16 cm) squares
- ☐ **colored or printed paper:** *6″ × 6″* (16 cm × 16 cm) squares
- ☐ **freezer paper (below)**
- ☐ **thread**
- ☐ **trims**

Helper Star Hint

FREEZER PAPER

You can find **freezer paper** in most grocery stores by the canning/freezing supplies or with the wax paper and aluminum foil. You can also buy it in sheets from your local quilt or craft store or online. It is used throughout this book for making patterns and stitching guides. Freezer paper is essential for the success of your beginning sewist: don't use a substitute.

SET?

1. Trace a shape onto the **DULL** side of the freezer paper. To download and print the shapes for easier tracing, refer to About This Book (page 5).

Trace.

2. Cut out the shape on the drawn lines.

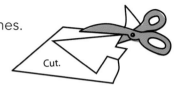
Cut.

3. Place the freezer-paper shape shiny side down on the paper square.

4. Set the iron to a cotton setting. Press for 5 seconds. The shape should stick to the paper. If it does not, press again.

Press.

5. Layer a paper square, 2 or 3 squares of paper towel, and the square with the freezer-paper shape.

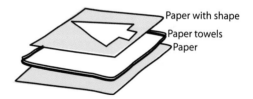
Paper with shape
Paper towels
Paper

Choose your favorite shapes
or make them all.

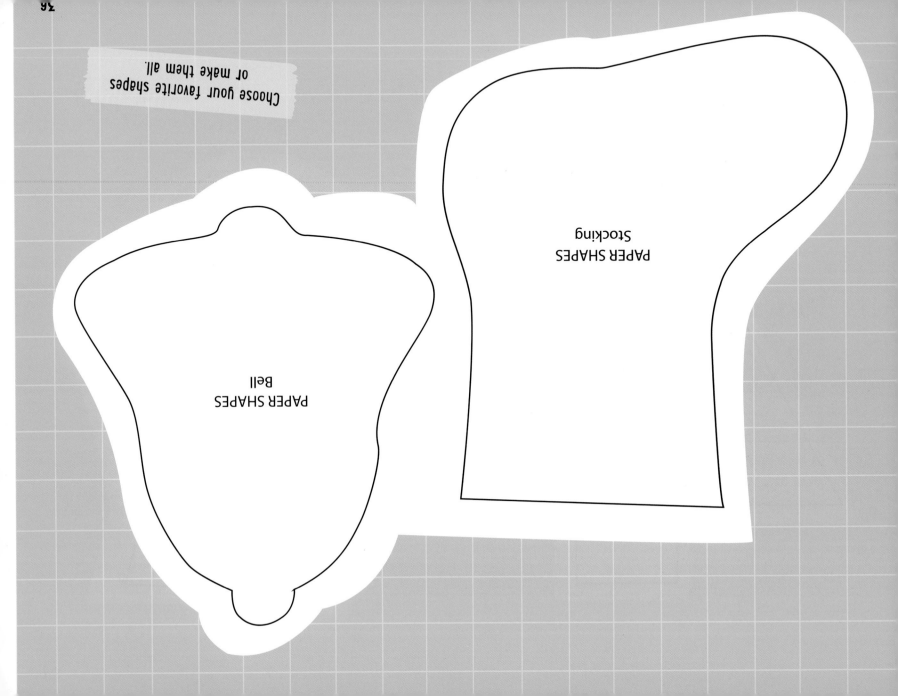

PAPER SHAPES
Stocking

PAPER SHAPES
Bell

Paper Shapes Are Fun!

Use them many ways. Can you think of any more creative ideas?

- Trim a tree.
- Use as present trim.
- Trim a window.
- Use as a greeting card.

PAPER SHAPES
Star

To Mom

Love, Kate

get WILD!

You're FIRST PLACE in our book!

Happy Birthday

WILDCARDS

These cards can be used as invitations, greeting cards, get well cards, or postcards with a first-class stamp. Discover a new fusing technique and how to stitch along an edge rather than on a line.

READY?

- ☐ **index cards**: 5″ × 8″ (14 cm × 20 cm)
- ☐ **scrap of fabric**: 6″ × 9″ (16 cm × 23 cm)
- ☐ **clear plastic**: 6″ × 9″ (16 cm × 23 cm)
- ☐ **paper-backed fusible web (page 29)**: 5″ × 8″ (14 cm × 20 cm)
- ☐ **wildcard fillers**: flat treasures such as sparkles, stickers, award ribbons, and photos
- ☐ **thread**
- ☐ **sewing basket (page 23)**

Helper Star Hint

Clear plastic, such as report covers or page protectors, is available in office supply stores.

SET?

1. Place the 5″ × 8″ piece of paper-backed fusible web, **PAPER** side up, on top of the index card, with all the edges even. Press for 8–10 seconds using a hot, dry iron. Peel off the paper backing.

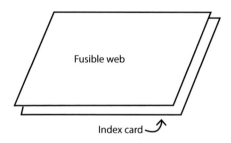

Fusible web

Index card

2. Layer in order on ironing board:

A. Fabric, **WRONG** side up

B. Fused index card, fusible side down

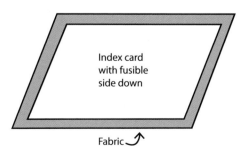

Index card with fusible side down

Fabric

3. Fuse the fabric and card together. Trim the fabric even with the index card.

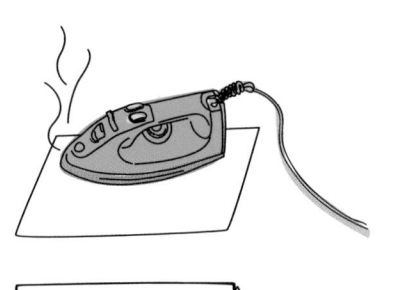

4. Place stickers, photos, ribbons, and other flat treasures on top of the fabric. Overlap the edges of the card if you want any of these sewn into place.

5. Center the clear plastic over the fabric side of card.

SEW!

1. With the clear plastic on top, stitch the layers together. The right-hand edge of the presser foot should be even with right-hand edge of card. Pivot at the corners. Begin and end the stitching as shown, leaving a few inches open.

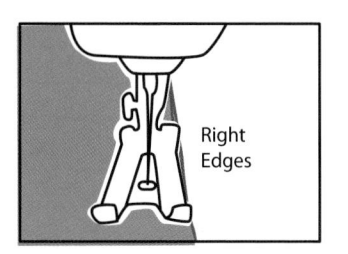

Right Edges

Opening

2. Fill the card with your sparkles, confetti, and other flat treasures. Be careful not to rip out any stitches.

Zoey

3. Finish the card by stitching the opening closed. Stitch over a few of your stitches at beginning and end to keep your threads from pulling out. Trim the plastic even with the card. Clip the thread ends close to the plastic.

Snip!

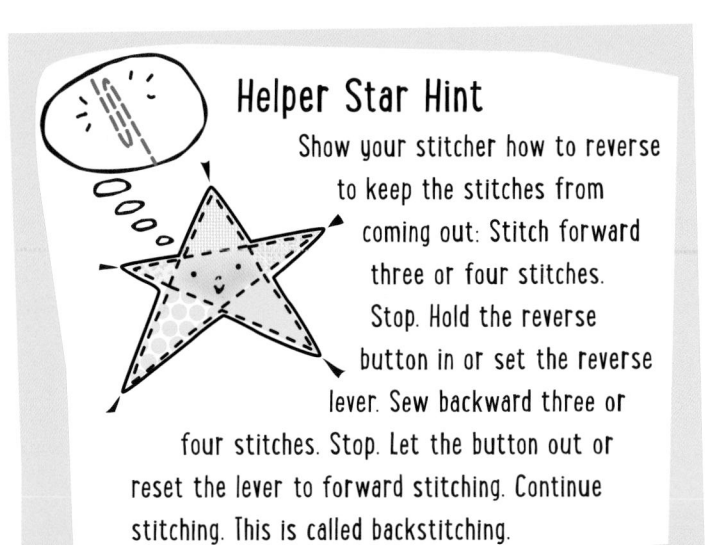

Helper Star Hint

Show your stitcher how to reverse to keep the stitches from coming out: Stitch forward three or four stitches. Stop. Hold the reverse button in or set the reverse lever. Sew backward three or four stitches. Stop. Let the button out or reset the lever to forward stitching. Continue stitching. This is called backstitching.

Use Your Wildest Imagination!

Make a special one-of-a-kind Wildcard.

Add to the Fun:

- ☐ BALLOONS
- ☐ CONFETTI
- ☐ GLITTER PAINT
- ☐ PHOTOS
- ☐ STICKERS
- ☐ TICKET STUBS
- ☐ GUM WRAPPERS
- ☐ SMALL ARTWORK
- ☐ RIBBONS
- ☐ PLAYING CARDS
- ☐ GIFT TAGS

Rhinoceros Wild Card

CRITICALLY ENDANGERED

- Rhinos may be thick skinned, but they are sensitive to sunburns.
- Rhinoceros are herbivores.
- They are FAST—running up to 40 miles per hour.
- Rhinos have bad eyesight but a great sense of smell and hearing.

Decorate the Back:

- ☐ STICKERS
- ☐ PERSONAL NOTES
- ☐ RUBBER STAMPINGS

SCIENTIFIC NAME: Diceros bicornis

DIET: Branches and leaves from shrubs and trees, some fruit, long grass, and herbs

LIFESPAN: 30–35 years

SIZE: Length: 7–10 feet; Height: About 4 feet

WEIGHT: About 1,500 pounds

HABITAT: Grasslands, savannas, shrublands, and deserts

RANGE: Sub-Saharan Africa

I think you are purrr-fect!

meow

CREATE A CARD

Make your own one-of-a-kind greeting cards and discover stitching around curves and corners. Make your first card using the heart shape (page 46).

READY?

- ☐ **scraps of fabric**: 4˝ × 5˝ (11 cm × 13 cm)

- ☐ **lightweight construction paper:** 8½˝ × 11˝ (22 cm × 28 cm)

- ☐ **paper-backed fusible web (page 29):** 4˝ × 5˝ (11 cm × 13 cm)

- ☐ **thread**

- ☐ **sewing basket (page 23)**

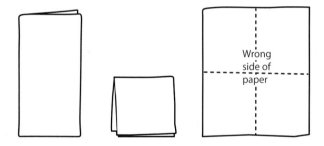

SET?

1. Carefully fold the construction paper in half. Fold it in half again. Crease. Unfold the paper so that the wrong side of the paper is facing up.

Wrong side of paper

2. Trace the heart onto the paper side of the fusible web. To download and print the shapes for easier tracing, refer to About This Book (page 5).

3. Place the rectangle with the traced heart on the bottom left corner of the wrong side of the card, paper side up. Keep the edges even. Press for 8–10 seconds using a hot, dry iron to fuse the web to the paper.

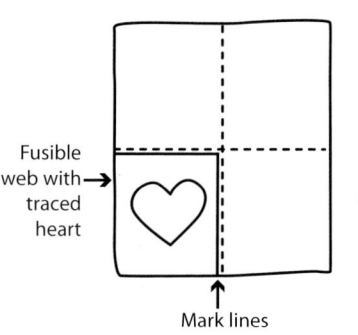

Fusible web with → traced heart

Mark lines

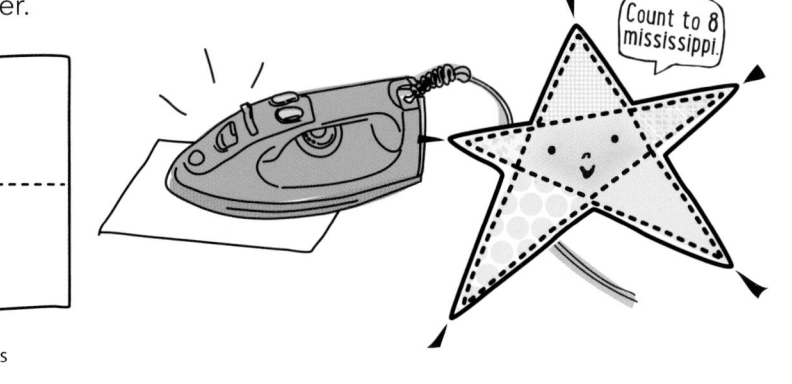

Count to 8 mississippi.

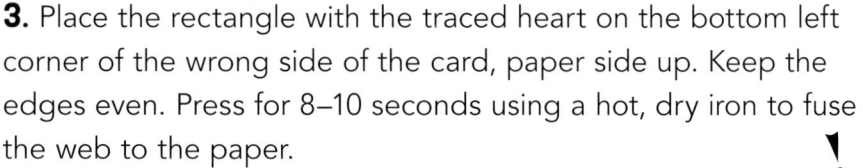

When do needles get along with each other?

You are so funny!

4. Poke scissors through the center of the heart and carefully cut it out to make a heart-shaped window. Carefully peel the paper backing off the fusible web that is around the window.

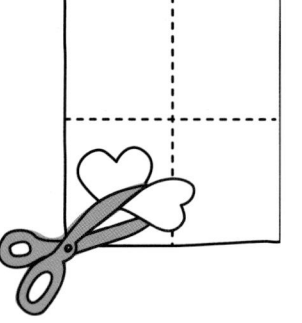

5. Place the 4″ × 5″ piece of fabric, with the **RIGHT** side facing the paper, over the fusible web. Press for 8–10 seconds to fuse the fabric to the card.

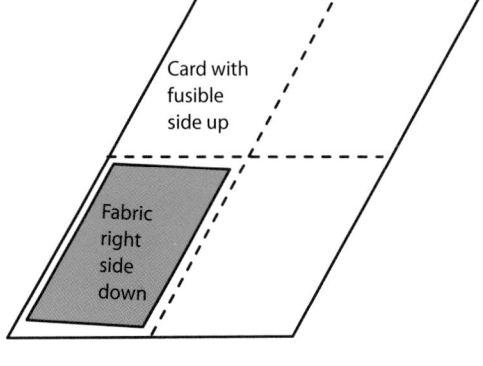

Card with fusible side up

Fabric right side down

6. Fold the card in half.

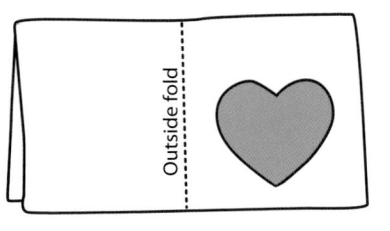

Outside fold

HA! HA! HA!

1. Stitch around the entire outside of the card, keeping the edge of the presser foot even with the edge of the card. Pivot at the corners. Remove the card and clip the threads.

2. Place the edge of the presser foot even with the side edge of the heart. Stitch around the entire heart. Pivot at the bottom point and the top inside point. Stitch over a few of your beginning stitches to keep them from coming out. Remove the card and clip the threads.

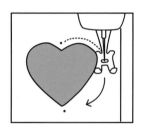
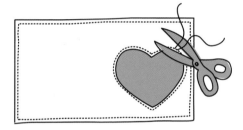

3. Personalize your card with glitter paints, marking pens, stickers, thumbprint designs, and a special message.

To Sam

Thank You for Helping.
Love,
Tracy

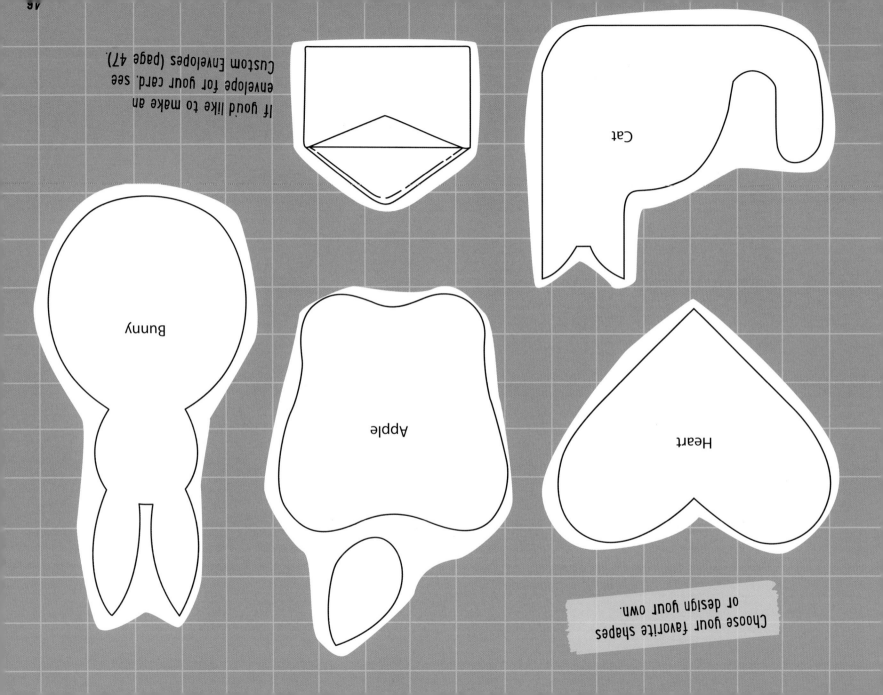

Cat

If you'd like to make an
envelope for your card, see
Custom Envelopes (page 47).

Bunny

Apple

Heart

Choose your favorite shapes
or design your own.

CUSTOM ENVELOPES

A perfect partner for your card! Choose a paper that folds easily and holds a crease.

1. Center your card in the middle of a square of paper. A bit of space should show between the card and the envelope paper.

2. Fold in the top and bottom of the envelope paper close to the card, and crease. Unfold.

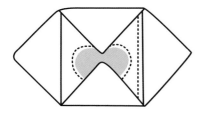

3. Fold in both sides close to the card, and crease. Unfold.

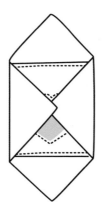

4. Set your card aside. Cut out the triangles formed from the folds.

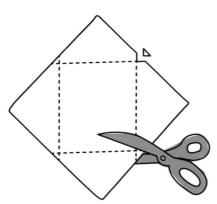

5. Fold up the bottom then the sides. Glue or tape along the edges.

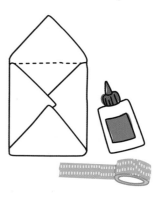

6. Put your card inside the envelope. Seal it with a fun sticker.

MACHINE T.L.C.

T.L.C. (Tender Loving Care) of Your Machine

Before you start the next project, it is a good idea to clean your machine and change your needle. To keep your machine happy, clean it regularly and replace the needle often. Consult your machine manual if you cannot figure something out.

Helper Star Hint

It may be necessary to consult your sewing machine manual for care and maintenance information. Walk through these directions with your beginning sewist.

1. Unplug your machine.

2. Remove the needle. Locate the thumbscrew or needle clamp to the upper right of the needle, and turn it until the needle is loose and can be pulled out. Do not replace the needle until you are through cleaning your machine.

3. Remove the presser foot. If the foot is connected to the shaft, it can be removed by loosening the screw or lever. It is usually located on the left side or behind the foot. Some machines have feet that pop off the shank—remove the foot by pushing down.

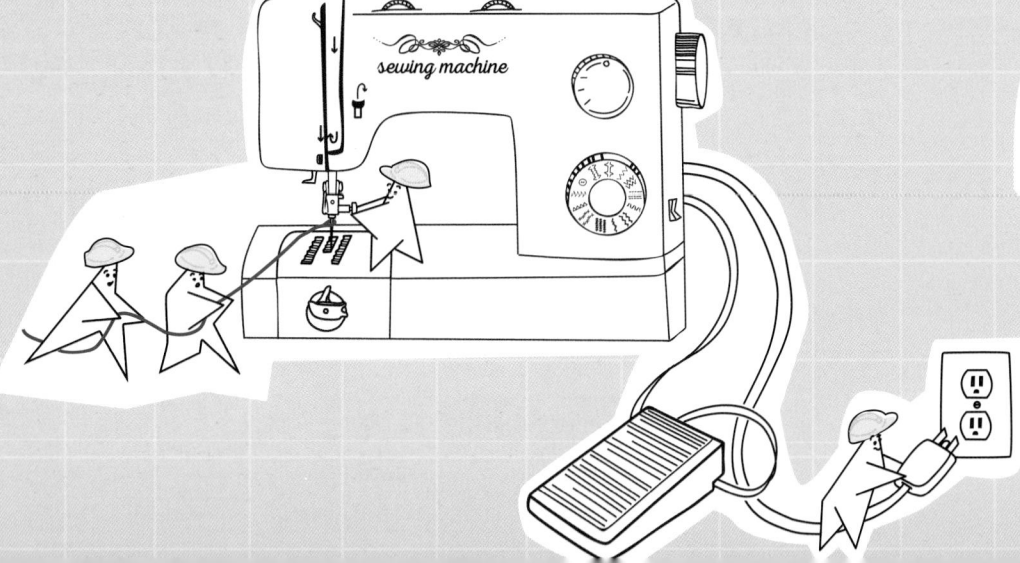

4. Remove the throat plate. Pop it off by pulling it forward, pushing it up, pushing it backward, or removing the screws holding it down using a screwdriver from your machine accessory box.

sewing machine

5. Remove the bobbin and bobbin case. There is usually a little lever to pull that releases the bobbin case.

6. Behind or underneath the bobbin case is the hook/race area. Ask your Helper Star to show you how to remove the race cover and hook.

7. Find the lint brush in your accessory box or use a clean paintbrush. Dust out the fuzz balls and dust bunnies that are around the feed dogs, bobbin case, and race. Don't let any of them escape from your clutches or they will clog your machine and eat your thread!

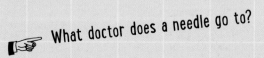
What doctor does a needle go to?

8. Use a clean, empty, **DRY** detergent bottle to blow out the baby dust bunnies. **SWOOSH** the air by squeezing the bottle with the tip directed toward the bobbin and feed dog area.

9. Have your Helper Star show you where to put a small drop of oil if needed.

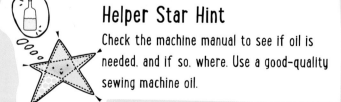
Helper Star Hint
Check the machine manual to see if oil is needed, and if so, where. Use a good-quality sewing machine oil.

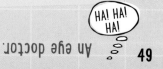
HA! HA! HA!

An eye doctor.

Putting It Back Together

1. Replace the hook/race. Turn the flywheel toward yourself to make sure the hook/race is properly in place.

2. Replace the bobbin in the bobbin case.

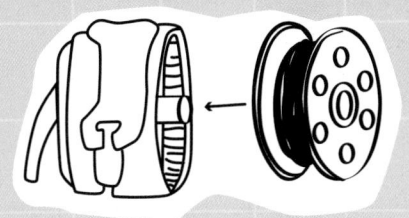

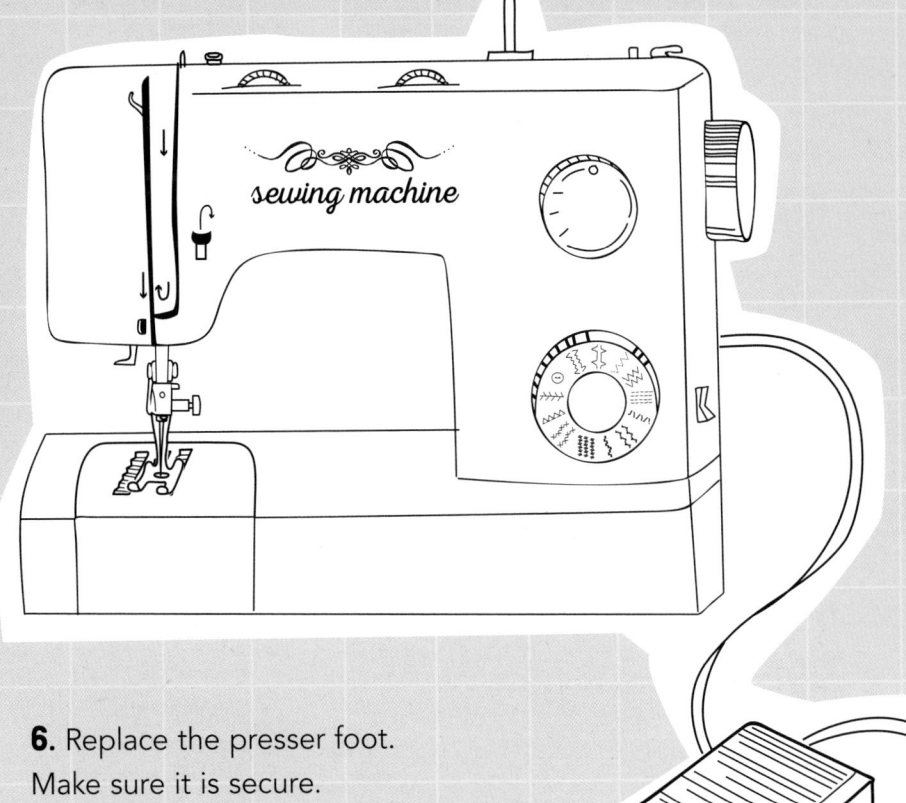

3. Put the bobbin case back in the machine. Secure with the lever.

4. Replace the throat plate. Make sure that it is firmly in place, or your needle will break.

5. Replace the needle. Be sure to place the flat side of the needle toward the back.

6. Replace the presser foot. Make sure it is secure.

7. Carefully plug in your machine.

8. Rethread the machine and stitch a test piece. If the machine does not stitch correctly, check top threading, bobbin threading, and bobbin case placement.

☞ Why does the needle go to the eye doctor?

HA! HA! HA!

Because it has thread in its eye.

50

MEASURE UP

If you were to pick up the tape measures one by one, taking the top one off each time, **in what order should you pick them up?** To download and print this page, refer to About This Book (page 5). To check your answer, see Puzzle Answers (page 124).

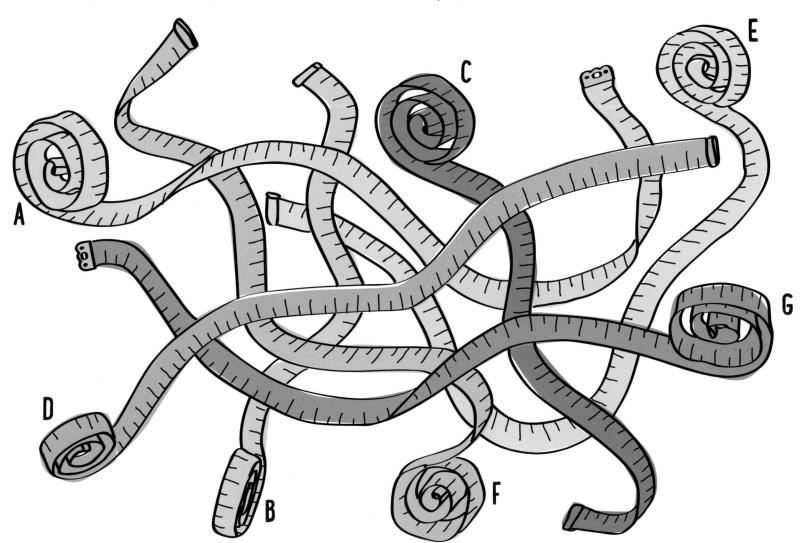

SOFT-SHAPE HEART

You are ready to discover stitching on fabric. Choose your favorite fun fabric combinations.

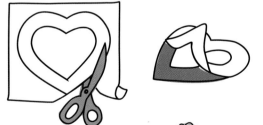

READY?

- ☐ **background fabric**: 2 squares 9″ × 9″ (23 cm × 23 cm)

- ☐ **heart fabric**: 1 square 9″ × 9″ (23 cm × 23 cm)

- ☐ **paper-backed fusible web (page 29)**: 1 square 9″ × 9″ (23 cm × 23 cm)

- ☐ **lightweight batting**: 1 square 9″ × 9″ (23 cm × 23 cm)

- ☐ **thread to match fabrics**

- ☐ **pinking scissors (optional)**

- ☐ **ribbon and/or adhesive-backed magnet for hanging**

- ☐ **sewing basket (page 23)**

SET?

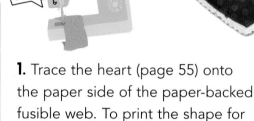

1. Trace the heart (page 55) onto the paper side of the paper-backed fusible web. To print the shape for easier tracing, refer to About This Book (page 5).

2. Place the traced heart, paper side up, onto the **WRONG** side of the heart fabric. Press for 8–10 seconds with a hot, dry iron to fuse. Cut out the heart on the drawn lines. Remove the paper backing, being careful not to stretch the heart out of shape.

3. Place 1 piece of background fabric on the ironing board **RIGHT** side up. Center the fused fabric heart, **RIGHT** side up, over the background fabric. Press for 8–10 seconds to fuse the heart to the background fabric.

53

4. Make a fabric sandwich by layering:

A. Other piece of background fabric, **WRONG** side up

B. Lightweight batting

C. Background with heart, **RIGHT** side up

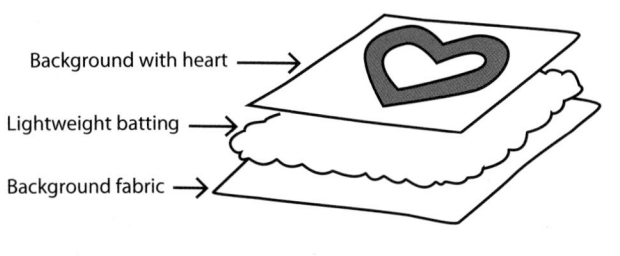

Background with heart ⟶

Lightweight batting ⟶

Background fabric ⟶

5. Pin the layers together.

SEW!

1. With thread to match the background, stitch *next to* the inside and outside edges of the heart. Stitch over a few of your first stitches to keep the threads from pulling out. Remove from the machine. Clip the threads.

2. With thread to match the heart, stitch *on top* of the heart along the inside and outside edges, lining up the presser foot with the edge of the heart.

3. Cut the background fabric ¼″ (.5 cm) away from the outside stitching line. Use pinking scissors if you have them.

4. If you like, attach a ribbon bow and write a special message with a permanent marker.

I MISS YOU!

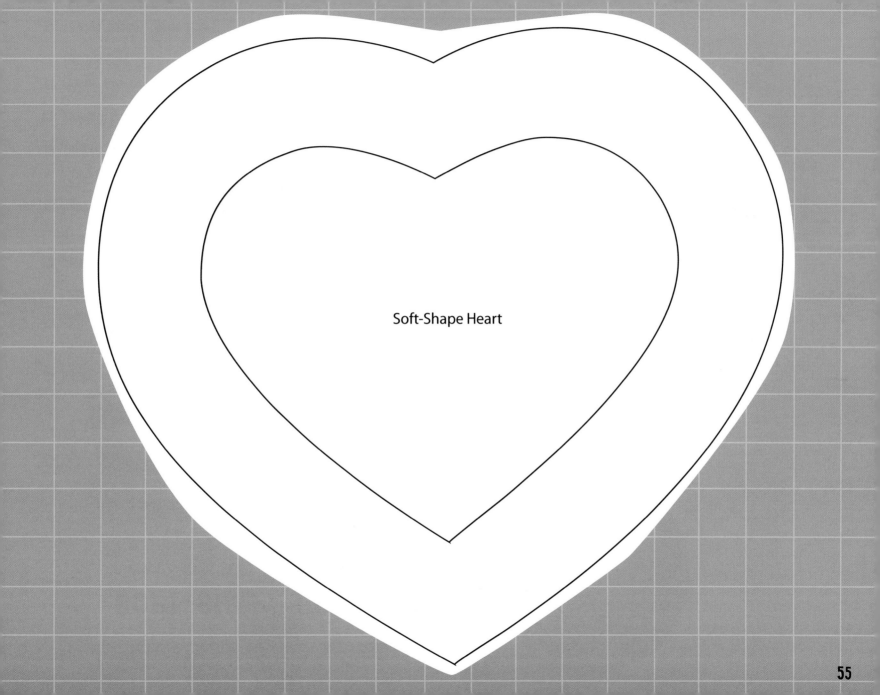

Soft-Shape Heart

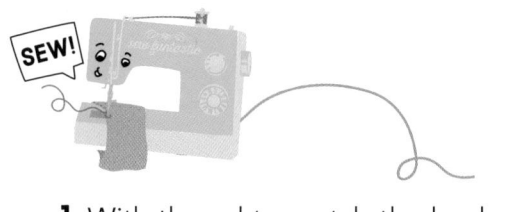

1. With thread to match the background, stitch *next to* the inside and outside edges of the peace sign. Stitch over a few of your first stitches to keep threads from pulling out. Remove from the machine. Clip the threads.

2. With thread to match the peace sign, stitch along the inside and outside edges *on top* of the peace sign, lining up the presser foot with the edge of the peace sign.

3. Cut the background fabric ¼″ (.5 cm) away from the outside stitching line. Use pinking scissors if you have them.

4. If you would like, attach a piece of ribbon or an adhesive-backed magnet on the back for hanging.

Helper Star Hint

If the machine zigzags, teach your sewist how to sew buttons on with the machine. Use the all-purpose or the zigzag presser foot. Widen the zigzag stitch until it is the width of the holes and shorten the stitch length to 0. Use the flywheel for the first few stitches. Stitch back and forth several times. Trim threads close to the button.

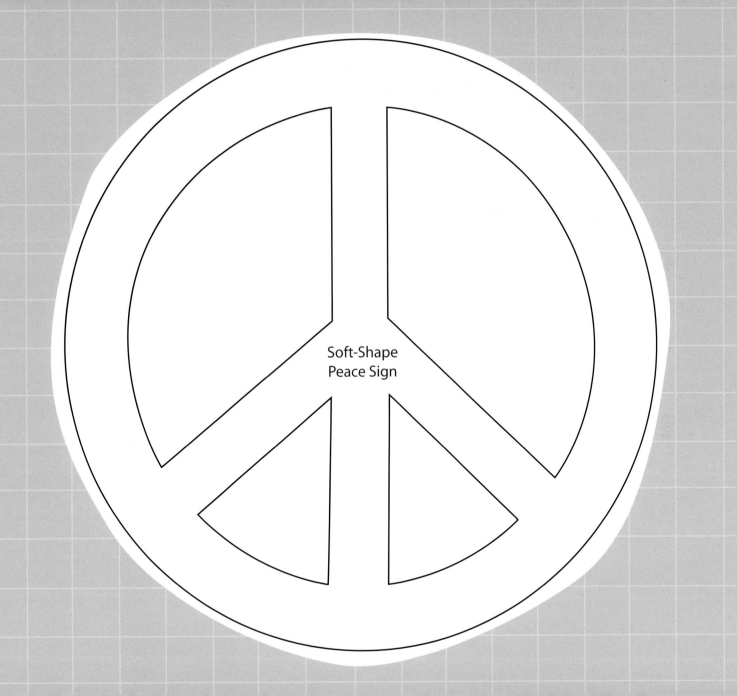

Soft-Shape
Peace Sign

BUTTON-UP OWL

Our panel of sewing experts (kids just like you) thought this was a terrific project. Choose your favorite shapes to make your very own original owl. Have fun!

- ☐ fabric scraps for owl parts and backings
- ☐ lightweight batting
- ☐ freezer paper (see Helper Star Hint, page 33)
- ☐ 2 flat buttons for wings
- ☐ 2 small buttons for eyes
- ☐ paper-backed fusible web (small amount for eyes) (page 29)
- ☐ thread
- ☐ pinking scissors (optional)
- ☐ sewing basket (page 23)

1. Choose the patterns you want to use to make your owl. You will need the owl body, head, ears, wings, eyes, talons, and beak. To download and print the patterns, refer to About This Book (page 5).

2. Trace the patterns onto the dull side of your freezer paper. Trace 1 body, 1 head, and 1 beak. Trace 2 ears, 2 wings, and 2 talons.

3. Cut out the shapes on the drawn lines.

4. Mix and match your fabric scraps for the owl parts. Place the shiny side of the patterns onto the **RIGHT** side of the fabric pieces.

5. Set the iron to a cotton setting. Press for 5 seconds. Shapes should stick to fabric. If they do not, press again.

6. Make fabric sandwiches for all the pieces except the eyes, by layering:

A. 1 piece of fabric, **WRONG** side up

B. Lightweight batting

C. Fabric with freezer-paper shape, **RIGHT** side up

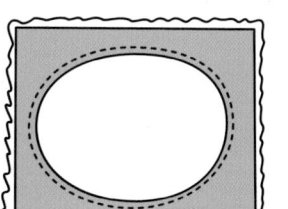

7. Pin the layers together.

8. Trace the eyes onto the paper side of the fusible web. Place the eye patterns, paper side up, onto the **WRONG** side of the chosen fabric. Press for 8–10 seconds using a hot, dry iron to fuse the eyes to fabric. Cut out the eyes on the drawn lines. Carefully remove the paper backing. Set the eyes aside.

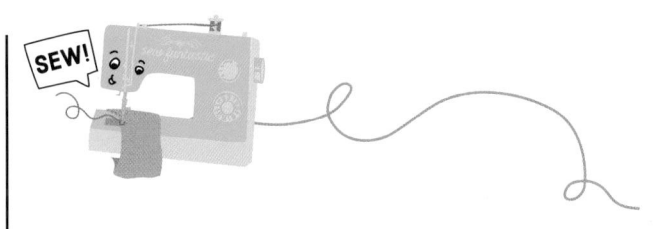

SEW!

1. Stitch next to the outside edge of each freezer-paper shape. Stitch over a few of your first stitches to keep threads from pulling out. Clip the threads.

2. Cut out the shapes ¼˝ (.5 cm) away from the stitching lines. Use pinking scissors if you have them.

3. Gently peel off the freezer-paper shapes.

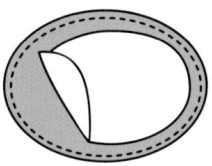

4. Pin the ears and talons to the back of the body. Use the photo (page 60) for placement. Tack the pieces in place by sewing a few stitches by hand or with the sewing machine, stitching forward and back over the same stitches.

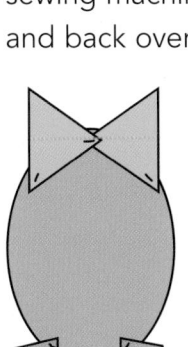

5. Place the eyes in position on the head and fuse them in place.

6. Pin the beak to the head. Tack the beak in place.

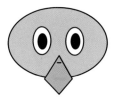

7. Pin the head and wings to the body. Hand or machine sew the buttons into position through all the layers on the wings and eyes.

Make your own original owl.

HOW DID YOU DO?

Look at your work closely to see how you are doing. **Fill out the checklist to see where you need more help.** To download and print the checklist, refer to About This Book (page 5).

	GREAT! Super Sewist	OKAY I need practice.	SO-SO I need help.
I traced my freezer-paper shapes carefully.			
I cut the shapes out smoothly.			
I accurately stitched next to the freezer paper.			
My cutting lines are ¼″ from the stitching lines.			
I started and ended with a backstitch.			
My backstitches were directly on top of my first stitches.			
My pivots are perfect.			
I slowed down for curves and stitched them carefully.			
I pivoted often around small curves.			
I sewed the buttons on firmly and neatly.			

CRAZY CORDS

Someone forgot to unplug one of these sewing machines. **Follow the cords to discover the culprit cord.** To download and print the page, refer to About This Book (page 5). To check your answer, see Puzzle Answers (page 124).

Always remember to unplug your machine when you are finished sewing.

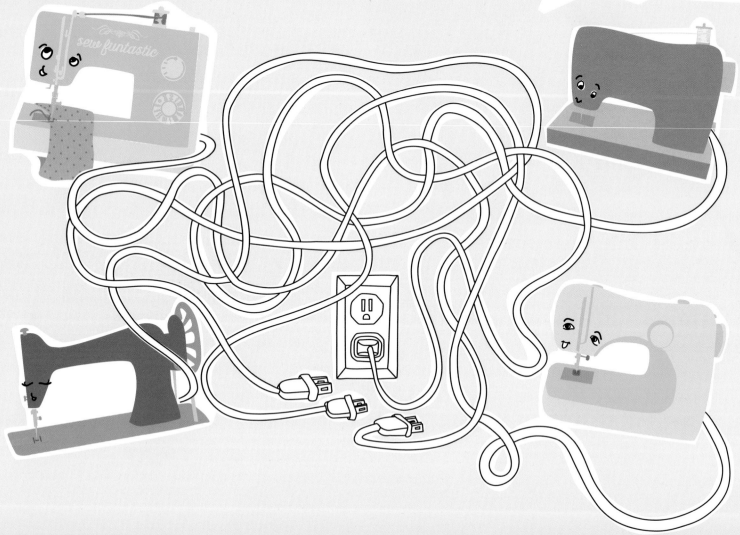

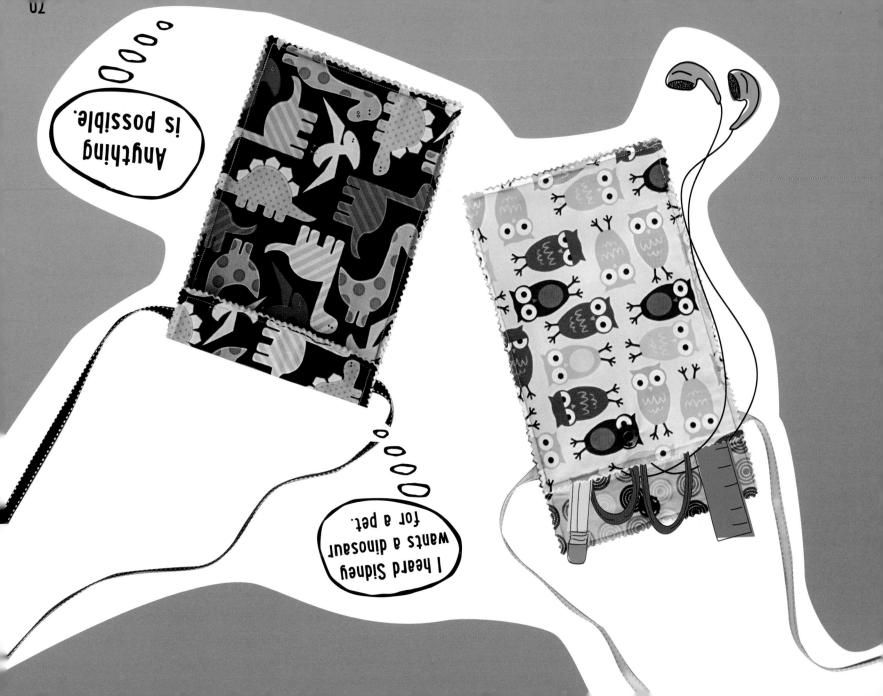

POSSIBILITIES POCKET

Learn how to make a pocket bag for your small electronics or special treasures…think of the possibilities.

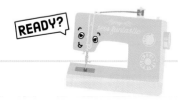

READY?

- [ ] **inside fabric**: 7″ × 10″ (18 cm × 26 cm) and 7″ × 12″ (18 cm × 31 cm)

- [ ] **outside fabric**: 7″ × 10″ (18 cm × 26 cm) and 7″ × 12″ (18 cm × 31 cm)

- [ ] **thin batting**: 7″ × 10″ (18 cm × 26 cm) and 7″ × 12″ (18 cm × 31 cm)

- [ ] **freezer paper** (see Helper Star Hint, page 33): 7″ × 10″ (18 cm × 26 cm) and 7″ × 12″ (18 cm × 31 cm)

- [ ] **grosgrain ribbon**: 1¼ yards (113 cm)

- [ ] **large snap or hook-and-loop dots**

- [ ] **thread**

- [ ] **pinking scissors** (optional)

- [ ] **sewing basket** (page 23)

Helper Star Hint

Hook-and-loop dots can be stitched on in place of snaps, but they should be stitched on after Sew, Step 3 (page 72), before the pocket is assembled.

SET?

1. Trace the patterns onto the dull side of freezer paper. To download and print the patterns, refer to About This Book (page 5). Cut the pattern pieces out on the drawn lines.

Front	Back

2. Place the shiny side of the patterns onto the **RIGHT** side of both outside fabric pieces. Set the iron to a cotton setting. Press for 5 seconds. The shapes should stick to the fabric. If they do not, press them again.

Ribbon placement

Ribbon placement

Snap placement

●

POSSIBILITIES POCKET
Front
Cut 1 from freezer paper.

SUPER SEWIST'S SECRET CODE 1

The positions of the lines and dots represent the letters of the alphabet. Use them to **decode the messages in this book**. To download and print the page, refer to About This Book (page 5). To check your answer, see Puzzle Answers (page 124).

a	b	c
d	e	f
g	h	i

j.	K.	l.
m.	n.	.o
p.	q.	r.

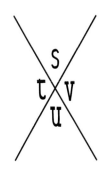

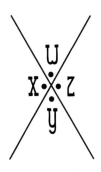

s u p _ _   _ _ _ _ _ _   _ _ _

_ _ _ _ _ _ _ _ _   _ _ _ _ _

_ _ _ _ _ _ _ _ _   _ _ _

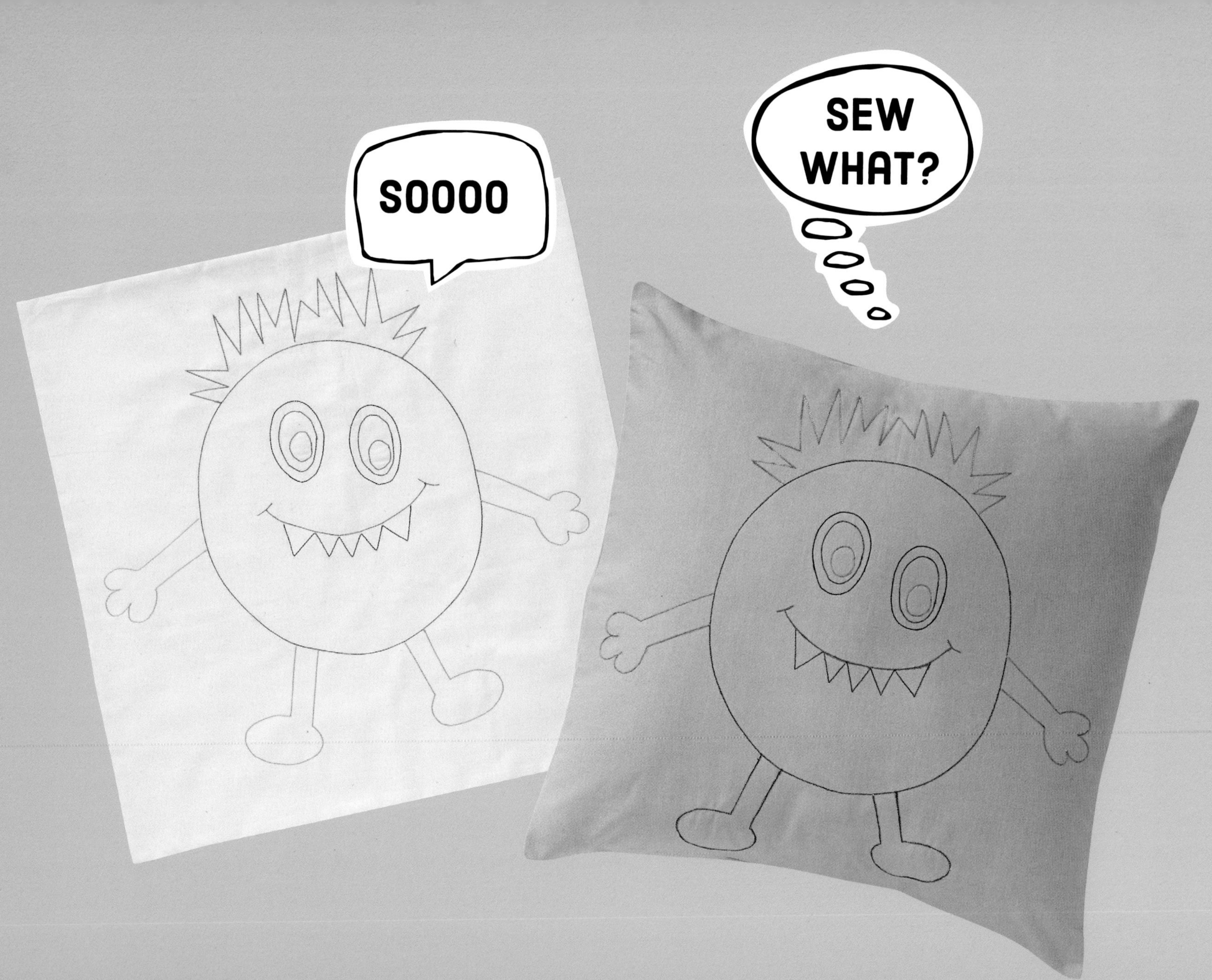
SOOOO
SEW WHAT?

MIX AND MATCH MONSTER

Did you know that you can draw with thread and the sewing machine?

READY?

- ◻ **solid-color cotton:** 2 squares 18″ × 18″ (46 cm × 46 cm)

- ◻ **backing fabric:** 1 square 18″ × 18″ (46 cm × 46 cm)

- ◻ **freezer paper (see Helper Star Hint, page 33):** 1 square 16″ × 16″ (40 cm × 40 cm)

- ◻ **polyester fiberfill for pillow (optional)**

- ◻ **several colors of thread or a spool of variegated thread**

- ◻ **white thread for the bobbin**

- ◻ **sewing basket (page 23)**

SET?

1. Fold the freezer paper in half. Place the fold of the freezer paper on the fold line of the monster body pattern. Trace half of the monster body. Flip the paper over and trace the other half. To download and print the patterns, refer to About This Book (page 5). Fold the monster body in half in the other direction to divide it into quarters.

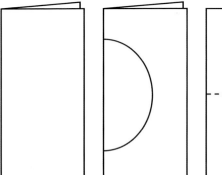

6. Turn the fabric **RIGHT** side out. Hold it by the corner and shake. Poke out the corners with a chopstick or dull pencil. Run the chopstick along the stitched seam to smooth it. Fold the unstitched opening to the inside and iron.

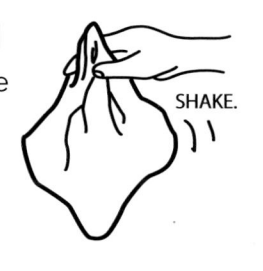

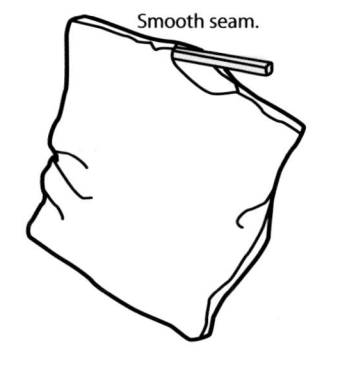

Smooth seam.

SHAKE.

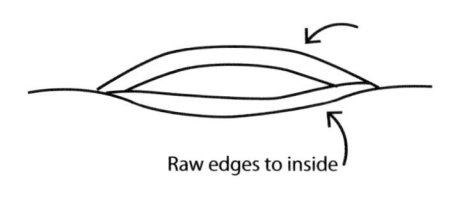

Raw edges to inside

7. TO MAKE A WALLHANGING: Stitch around the fabric with the right-hand side of the presser foot even with the edge of the fabric. This is called topstitching.

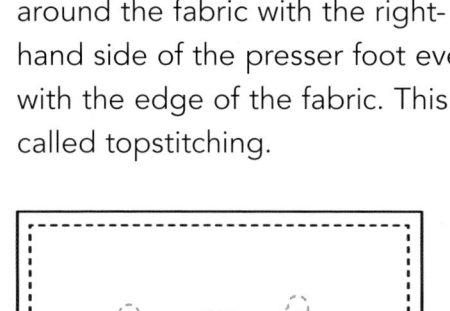

8. TO MAKE A PILLOW: Stuff polyester fiberfill into the pillow through the opening you left for turning. Try to keep it soft and even, not hard and lumpy! It usually works best to put in small amounts of stuffing at a time. Start with the corners first, and then fill the rest of the pillow. Turn in the raw edges of the opening, and pin. Stitch closed by hand. This is called a whipstitch.

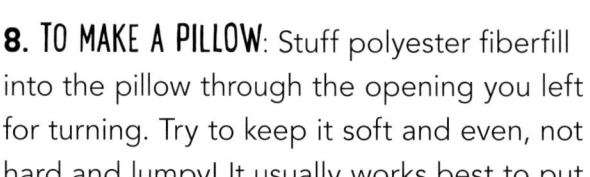

Remember This Point!

To find the 1/2" seam allowance, place a ruler under the presser foot. Put the needle on the 1/2" mark. Place a piece of masking tape along the edge of the ruler. You may find this line already marked on your throat plate.

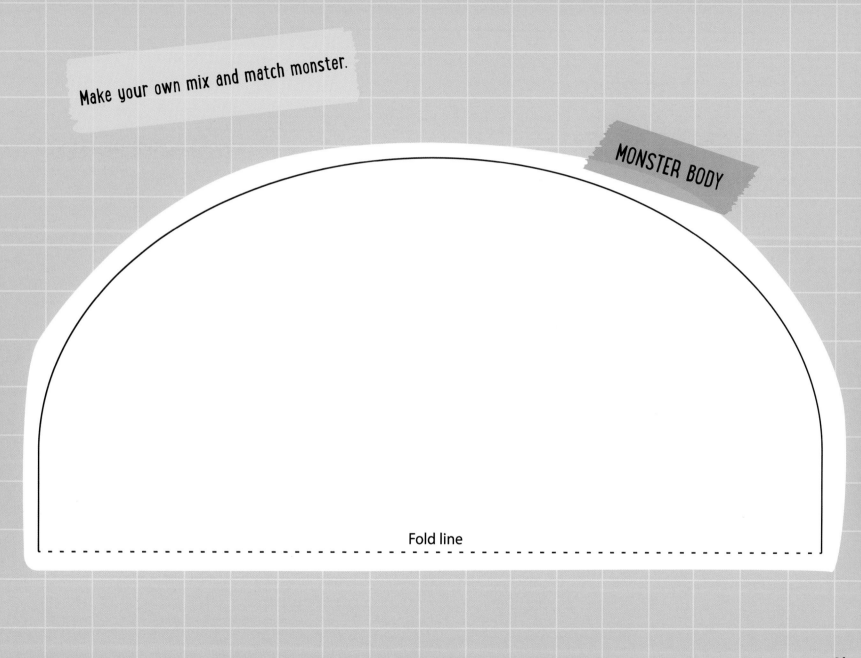

Make your own mix and match monster.

MONSTER BODY

Fold line

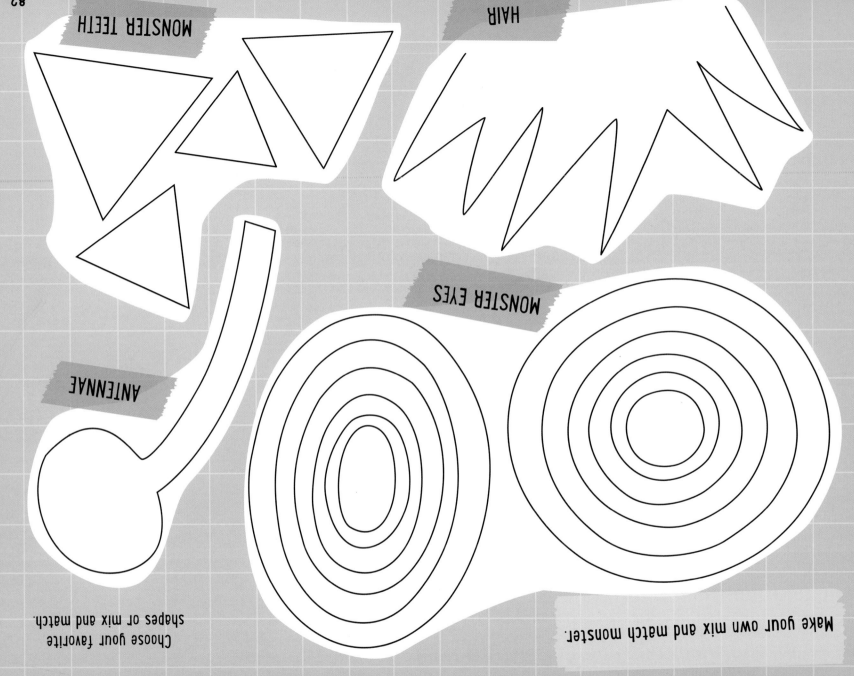

MONSTER TEETH

HAIR

ANTENNAE

MONSTER EYES

Choose your favorite
shapes or mix and match.

Make your own mix and match monster.

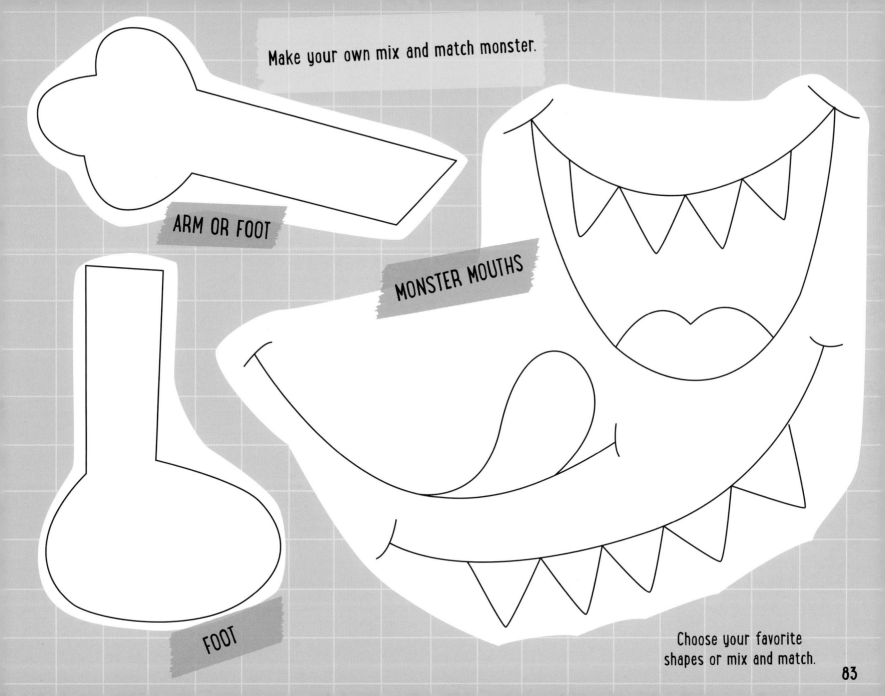

Make your own mix and match monster.

ARM OR FOOT

MONSTER MOUTHS

FOOT

Choose your favorite
shapes or mix and match.

Make your own mix and match monster.

FRED'S THREAD

Fred threaded a needle with red thread. **Who's Fred?** To download and print the page, refer to About This Book (page 5). To check your answer, see Puzzle Answers (page 124).

COVER-UPS

Would you like to cover a notebook, a school book, or a paperback? Choose a bright, fun print or find a fabric that represents a subject, like numbers for a math book.

READY?

- cotton fabric for cover: ½ yard (.5 m)
- cotton fabric for pocket: 7″ × 9″ (17.5 cm × 22.5 cm)
- book or notebook no larger than a 3-ring binder with a 3″ spine
- heavy or craft-weight iron-on interfacing: 1 yard (1 m)
- thread
- ruler or yardstick
- sewing basket (page 23)

Remember This Point!

To finger-press, fold the interfacing in half on a flat surface and run your finger along the fold. Open it out. Use this center crease as a guideline to match up to the centerline on the fabric.

SET?

1. Place the interfacing on a table. Hold your book by the pages and let the front and back covers fall onto the table. Gently push down to make the cover as flat as possible.

2. Trace around the cover.

3. Cut out the interfacing on the drawn line. Fold it in half and finger-press the center crease.

1. Stitch along the sides and bottom of the pocket. Backstitch at the beginning and end, and pivot at corners.

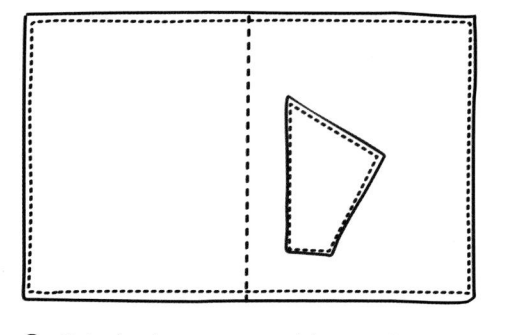

2. Stitch the pressed hem down around the entire outside edge of the book cover.

3. Place the book cover on a table with the interfaced side up. Fold short ends under ⅛″ from the interfacing. Be sure the top and bottom edges are even. Pin.

4. Stitch the top and bottom edges about ⅛″ away from the interfacing. Remember to backstitch.

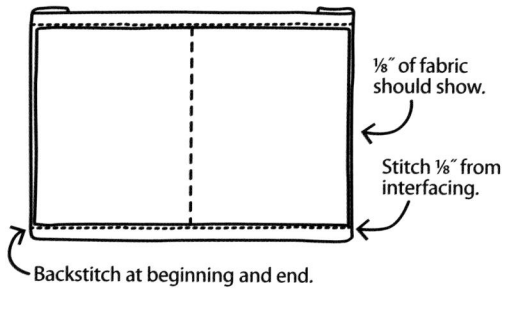

⅛″ of fabric should show.

Stitch ⅛″ from interfacing.

Backstitch at beginning and end.

5. Turn the book cover right side out. Carefully push out the corners using a chopstick or dull pencil.

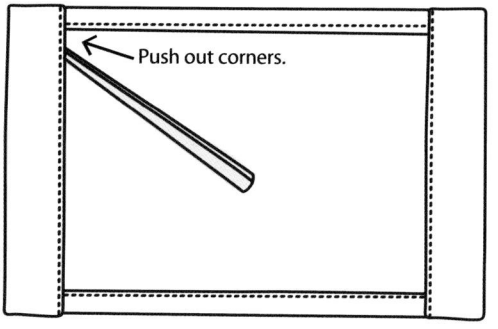

Push out corners.

6. Hold your book by the pages, letting the covers drop down. Put each cover into an end. If you have a pocket, make sure it is on the front. Carefully slide the cover onto the book.

Now you can cover all of your books and notebooks with fun fabrics!

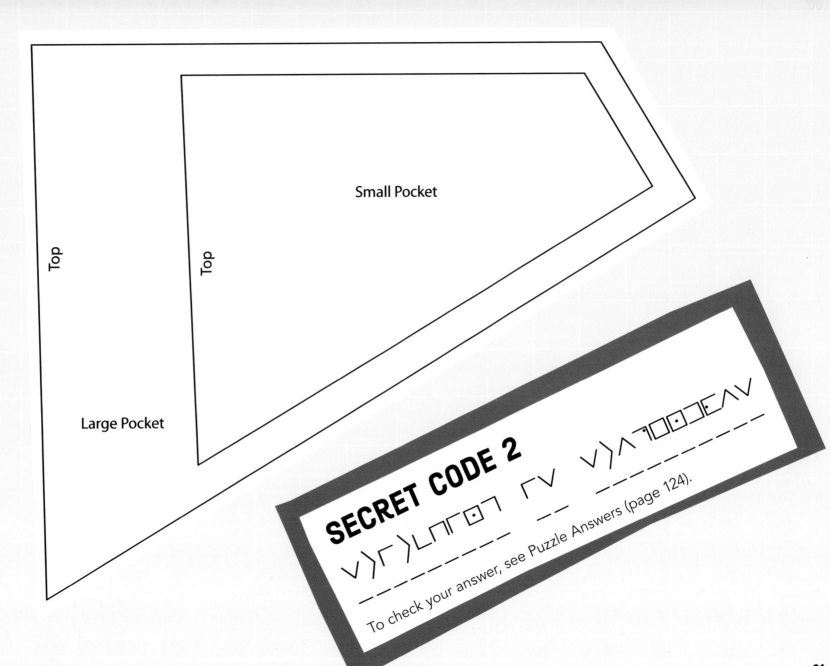

Top

Top

Small Pocket

Large Pocket

SECRET CODE 2

∨⟩⌐⟩∟⌐⌐•⌐ ⌐∨ ∨⟩∧ˀ⊓⊓⊡•⊐∈∧∨

_ _

To check your answer, see Puzzle Answers (page 124).

UP WITH LETTERS

Sewing terms are shown with their vowels in place. Choose your consonants from the list below. Cross off each consonant as you use it. To download and print the puzzle, refer to About This Book (page 5). To check your answers, see Puzzle Answers (page 124).

WORD BANK

IRONING BOARD	BOBBIN
PRESS	SCISSORS
SEWING BASKET	FLYWHEEL
FABRIC	PIVOT
PINCUSHION	PENCIL
THROAT PLATE	TAPE MEASURE
PRESSER FOOT	RULER
BUTTONS	THREAD
LIGHT	SEAM RIPPER
PINS	FOOT PEDAL
FEED DOGS	NEEDLE
RIBBON	

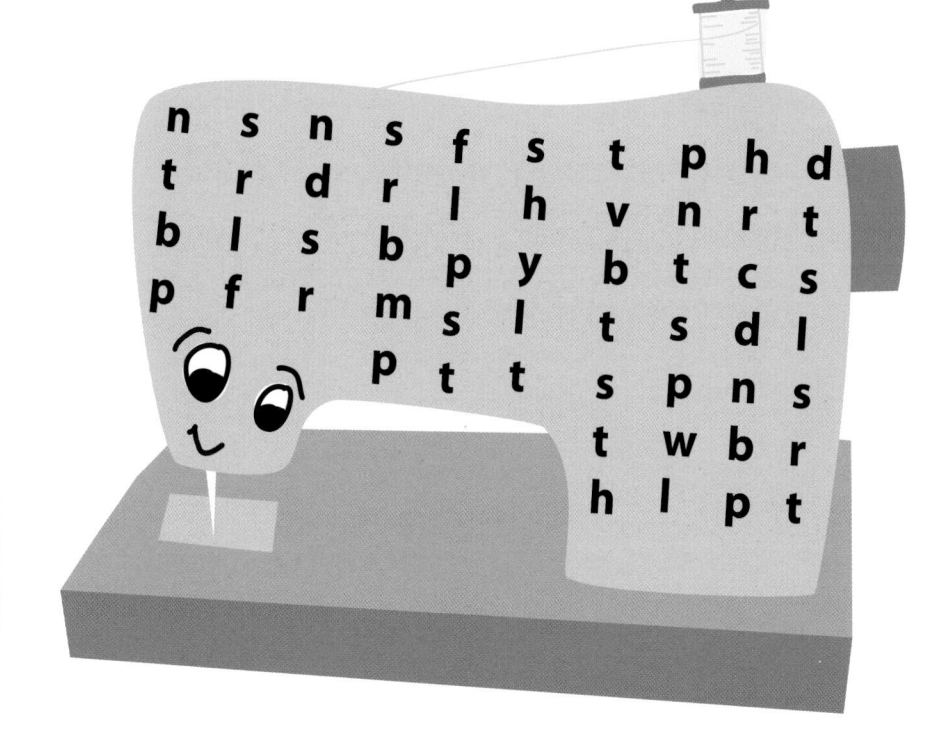

1. _ o _ _ i _

2. _ a _ e   _ e a _ u _ e

3. _ _ _ o a _   _ _ a _ e

4. _ _ _ e a _

5. _ _ i _ _ o _ _

6. _ _ e _ _

7. _ u _ _ o _ _

8. _ i _ _

9. _ _ _ _ _ _ e e _

10. _ o o _   _ e _ a _

11. _ i _ o _

12. _ e e _ _ e

FISH 'N STITCH

Stitch along the line and see if you can catch a fish!

To download and print the page, refer to About This Book (page 5).

☞ If fish travel in schools, how does thread travel?

Start

End

HA! HA! HA!

In spools! 93

BACKPACK

Learn how to make a backpack for carrying your school books and supplies.

- ◻ **cotton fabric for outside, 42″ wide:**
  ½ yard (½ m)

- ◻ **cotton fabric for lining, 42″ wide:**
  ½ yard (½ m)

- ◻ **cording: 4 yards (4 m)**

- ◻ **large safety pin**

- ◻ **thread**

- ◻ **sewing basket (page 23)**

1. Cut the outside and lining fabrics into rectangles 16″ × 32″ (40.6 cm × 81.3 cm).

2. Cut the cording into 2 pieces, each 2 yards (2 m) long.

3. Place the outside and lining pieces **RIGHT** sides together. Pin the layers together.

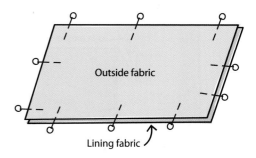

Outside fabric

Lining fabric

Helper Star Hint
The cording should be soft and pliable so that it is easy to stitch through.

SEWING SILLIES

Name the items by combining the names of the pictures. To download and print the page, refer to About This Book (page 5). To check your answers, see Puzzle Answers (page 124).

☞ What kind of fish does a bird sit on?

A perch.

DON'T LET UP!

Can you stitch this shape without lifting the needle from the paper and without double-stitching any line?

Remember that there may be more than one answer. Trace the design on copy paper, copy on a copier, or download and print. (Refer to About This Book, page 5.) To check your answer, see Puzzle Answers (page 124).

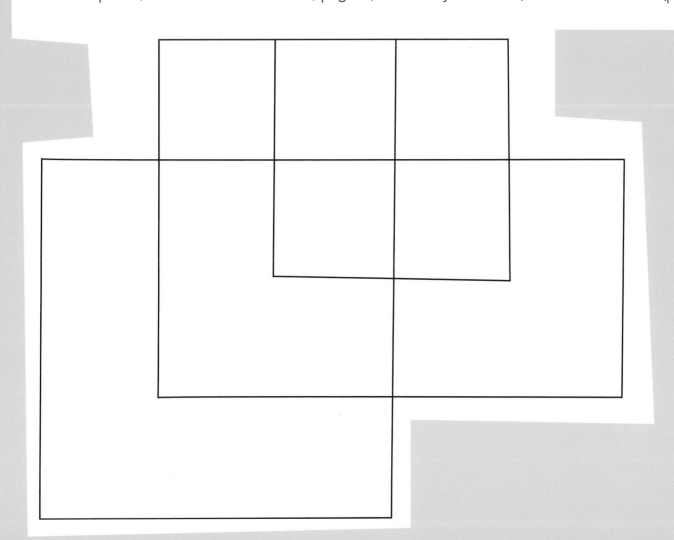

BAG IT

What a treat for you (and Mother Earth) to take your lunch in your very own insulated reusable bag! Make one for yourself and then have fun choosing other fabric combinations to make unique gifts for your friends.

- ☐ **cotton fabric for bottom**: ⅙ yard (.2 m)
- ☐ **cotton fabric for middle**: ⅙ yard (.2 m)
- ☐ **cotton fabric for top**: ⅙ yard (.2 m)
- ☐ **thin batting, 45″ wide**: ⅓ yard (.3 m) or

  Insul-Fleece (C&T Publishing): 1 package (27″ × 45″, 69 cm × 114 cm)
- ☐ **freezer paper (see Helper Star Hint, page 33): 2 pieces 6″ × 12″** (15 cm × 30 cm)
- ☐ **thread to match top fabric**
- ☐ **sewing basket (page 23)**

SET?

1. Fold the freezer paper in half, to 6″ × 6″. Place the fold of the freezer paper on the fold line of the pattern piece. Trace the pattern. To download and print the patterns for easier tracing, refer to About This Book (page 5). With the paper still folded, cut it out. Save the other piece of freezer paper for making the corner pattern.

Fold.

Trace.

Cut.

2. Pin the pattern to the bottom fabric and cut 4. Pin the pattern to the middle fabric and cut 4. Pin the pattern to the top fabric and cut 4. Pin the pattern to the batting or Insul-Fleece and cut 6. Lay out the pieces as shown, with the **WRONG** sides together. Place the batting or Insul-Fleece between each 2 pieces to make 3 layers in each section.

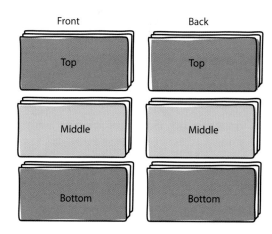

Front — Back

Top — Top

Middle — Middle

Bottom — Bottom

12. Peel off the freezer paper, turn the bag right side out, and push out the corners.

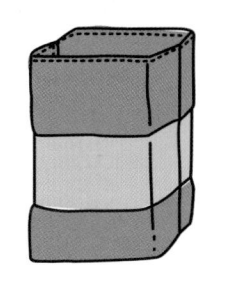

13. Turn the top edge of the bag to the inside on the stitched line. Stitch the hem in place.

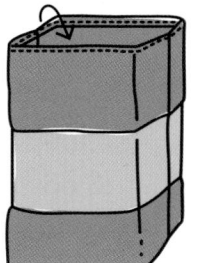

Pack your lunch and enjoy all the compliments you will receive. ☺

Fold line

Trace 2 on freezer paper.

BAG IT
Corner Pattern

BAG IT
Bag Pattern

WORD SEARCH 2

Hidden in the puzzle below are the 19 sewing machine parts that you know. For an even bigger challenge, cover the list and then do the search. To download and print the puzzle, refer to About This Book (page 5). To check your answers, see Puzzle Answers (page 124).

```
R E T F I L T O O F R E S S E R P
Z E S D F G T R L P K L I O T F R
A W V K J Q T Y E E P T E C F U E
E S R E U W W H N V M R L X O B S
T E T I R H G N G D I F D W O N S
A P V F E S K J T X O V E S T M E
L U B E Y Z E M H G L B E D P L R
P E L E B O B B I N W I N D E R F
T K I D J K L O U P M H J R D L O
A A G D D N A B Z T C F B H A N O
O T H O H I Y B L J T N F M L I T
R D T G T B H I J K L O M O I P K
H A B S D B X N A S W Q N R N L H
T E N S I O N C O N T R O L K O Z
R R Y J W B M A N B P L K F G O R
H H K M N D S S W R T U P K L P G
A T Q W T H R E A D G U I D E S F
```

presser foot lifter

presser foot

reverse button

bobbin winder

bobbin case

tension control

feed dogs

throat plate

bobbin

needle

flywheel

thread take-up

thread guides

light

foot pedal

spool pin

on/off

length

width

☞ If a cow went to school, what would be her favorite subject?

Moosic!

HA! HA! HA!

105

Ingredients:

mmm... cheese

BURGER BITES

Practice your newfound skills and learn some new ones when making this yummy burger, including a bit of patchwork, turning and stuffing, whipstitching a seam closed, fusing and stitching through freezer paper, machine quilting through batting, and making fabric yo-yos.

SET?

READY?

COTTON FABRIC:

- ❑ 2 squares 6″ × 6″ (15 cm × 15 cm) brown for burger

- ❑ 2 squares 6″ × 6″ (15 cm × 15 cm) beige for inside bun

- ❑ 1 rectangle 6″ × 18″ (15 cm × 46 cm) tan for outside bun

- ❑ 2 squares 6″ × 6″ (15 cm × 15 cm) red for tomato

- ❑ 2 squares 6″ × 6″ (15 cm × 15 cm) white for onion

- ❑ 2 squares 6″ × 6″ (15 cm × 15 cm) yellow for cheese

- ❑ 2 rectangles 7″ × 14″ (18 cm × 36 cm) green for lettuce

- ❑ 3 squares 6″ × 6″ (15 cm × 15 cm) green for pickles

- ❑ polyester stuffing

- ❑ thin batting: 7 squares 6″ × 6″ (15 cm × 15 cm)

- ❑ freezer paper (see Helper Star Hint, page 33): 18″ × 28″ (46 cm × 71 cm)

- ❑ paper-backed fusible web (page 29): 7″ × 14″ (18 cm × 36 cm)

- ❑ thread to match fabrics plus purple for the onion

- ❑ pinking scissors (optional)

- ❑ sewing basket (page 23)

1. Trace all the patterns onto freezer paper. To download and print the patterns, refer to About This Book (page 5). Be sure to trace 2 lettuce, 3 pickle, and 4 top bun shapes. Trace all the markings as well.

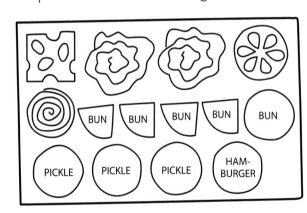

2. Cut the shapes out. Cut the circles out of the cheese pattern.

Cheese and Lettuce

1. Place the shiny side of the cheese and lettuce freezer-paper shapes onto the **RIGHT** side of the fabrics. Leave ½″ between the lettuce pieces.

2. Set the iron to a cotton setting and press for 5 seconds. If the shapes do not stick, press again.

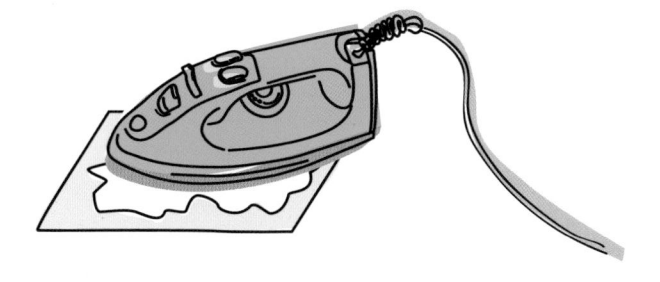

Tomato, Onion, Hamburger, Pickles, and Tan Outside Bun

1. Place the shiny side of the freezer-paper shapes onto the **WRONG** side of the fabrics. Leave ½″ between the shapes if they are on the same piece of fabric.

2. Press for 5 seconds. If shapes do not stick, press again.

Hamburger and Bottom Bun

1. LAYER IN ORDER FOR HAMBURGER:

A. 2 pieces of batting

B. 1 piece of hamburger fabric, **RIGHT** side up

C. Fabric with freezer-paper shape, **WRONG** side up

HAMBURGER

2. LAYER IN ORDER FOR BOTTOM BUN:

A. 2 pieces of batting

B. Beige fabric, **RIGHT** side up

C. Tan fabric with freezer-paper shape, **WRONG** side up

BUN

3. Stitch around the circles, leaving an opening to turn. Remember to backstitch. Trim ¼″ from the stitched line.

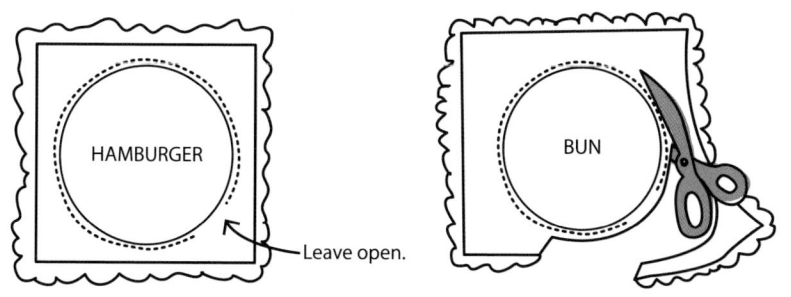

HAMBURGER — Leave open.

BUN

4. Peel off the freezer paper. Turn the circles right side out—batting will turn to inside.

5. Push out the seam allowances with a chopstick or dull pencil until the edges are smooth.

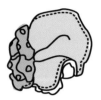

6. Stuff a small amount of stuffing between the layers of batting.

7. Whipstitch (Sew, Step 8, page 80) openings closed by hand with matching thread.

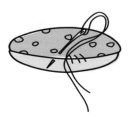

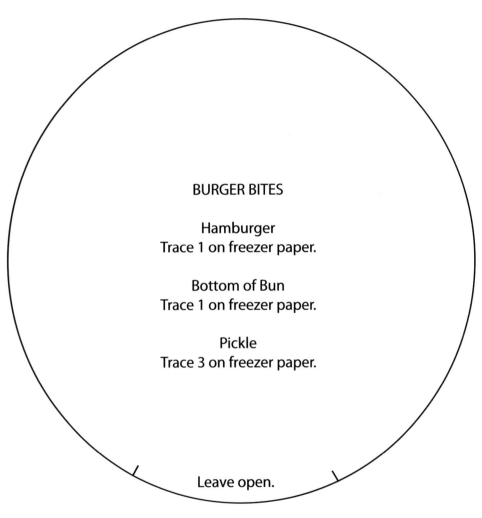

BURGER BITES

Hamburger
Trace 1 on freezer paper.

Bottom of Bun
Trace 1 on freezer paper.

Pickle
Trace 3 on freezer paper.

Leave open.

Pickles

1. Cut out the fabric about ¼″ beyond the freezer-paper circles.

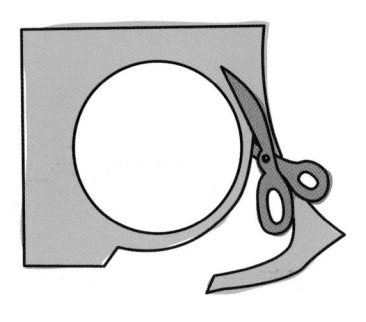

2. Press the fabric edge over the freezer-paper circles. Peel off the freezer paper.

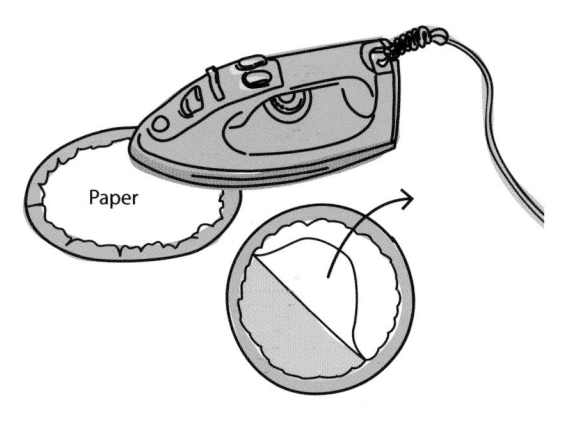

Paper

3. Thread a needle with 2 strands of thread and knot the end. Stitch down the folded-over edge of each circle with a long running stitch.

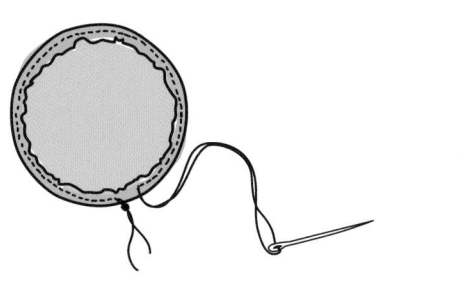

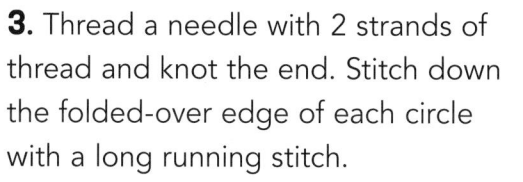

4. Pull up the threads gently but tightly to gather the circle. Knot off the thread. Flatten into a circular shape. This is called a yo-yo.

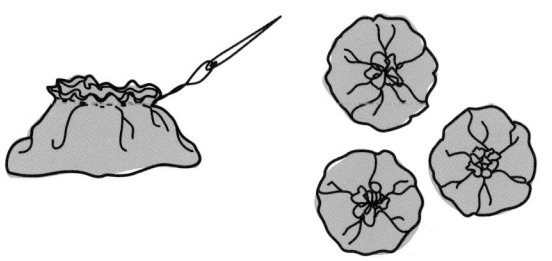

Pic

Knock. knock.

Who's there?

Lettuce.

Lettuce who?

HA! HA! HA!

Lettuce make a hamburger.

Top of Bun

1. Place 2 top bun pieces **RIGHT** sides together, matching all the edges. Stitch along one straight edge. Open up the 2 pieces and press the seam to one side.

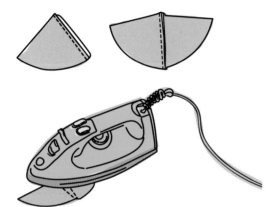

2. Repeat Step 1 for the other 2 pieces.

3. Place the 2 sections **RIGHT** sides together and stitch to make the top bun circle. Press the seam to one side.

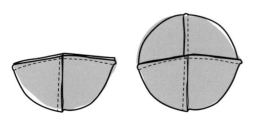

4. Place the top bun circle **RIGHT** side down on the square of beige bun fabric that is **RIGHT** side up. Pin.

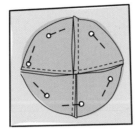

5. Stitch around the circle, with the edge of presser foot even with the edge of the circle. Leave an opening for turning. Trim next to the top bun.

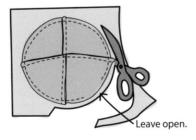
Leave open.

6. Turn the circle right side out and push out the seam allowances until smooth, using a chopstick as needed.

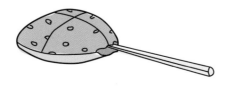

7. Stuff softly to create a rounded bun shape.

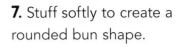

Whipstitch (Sew, Step 8, page 80) the opening closed by hand with matching thread.

BURGER BITES
Top of Bun
Trace 4 on
freezer paper.

Lettuce

1. Place the 7″ × 14″ piece of lettuce fabric **WRONG** side up on the ironing board. Place the paper-backed fusible web, paper side up, on the fabric. Keep the edges even. Press for 8–10 seconds using a hot, dry iron. Peel off the paper backing.

2. Place second piece of lettuce fabric with freezer-paper shapes, **RIGHT** side up, over the web. Press for 8–10 seconds.

3. Cut the lettuce pieces apart, leaving at least a ¼″ seam allowance around each piece.

4. Stitch around the freezer-paper pattern, following the direction of the arrow and ending up in the middle. Set the stitch length to a shorter stitch to make it easier to tear off the freezer paper.

5. Peel off the freezer paper. Trim around the outer stitching line with pinking scissors if you have them.

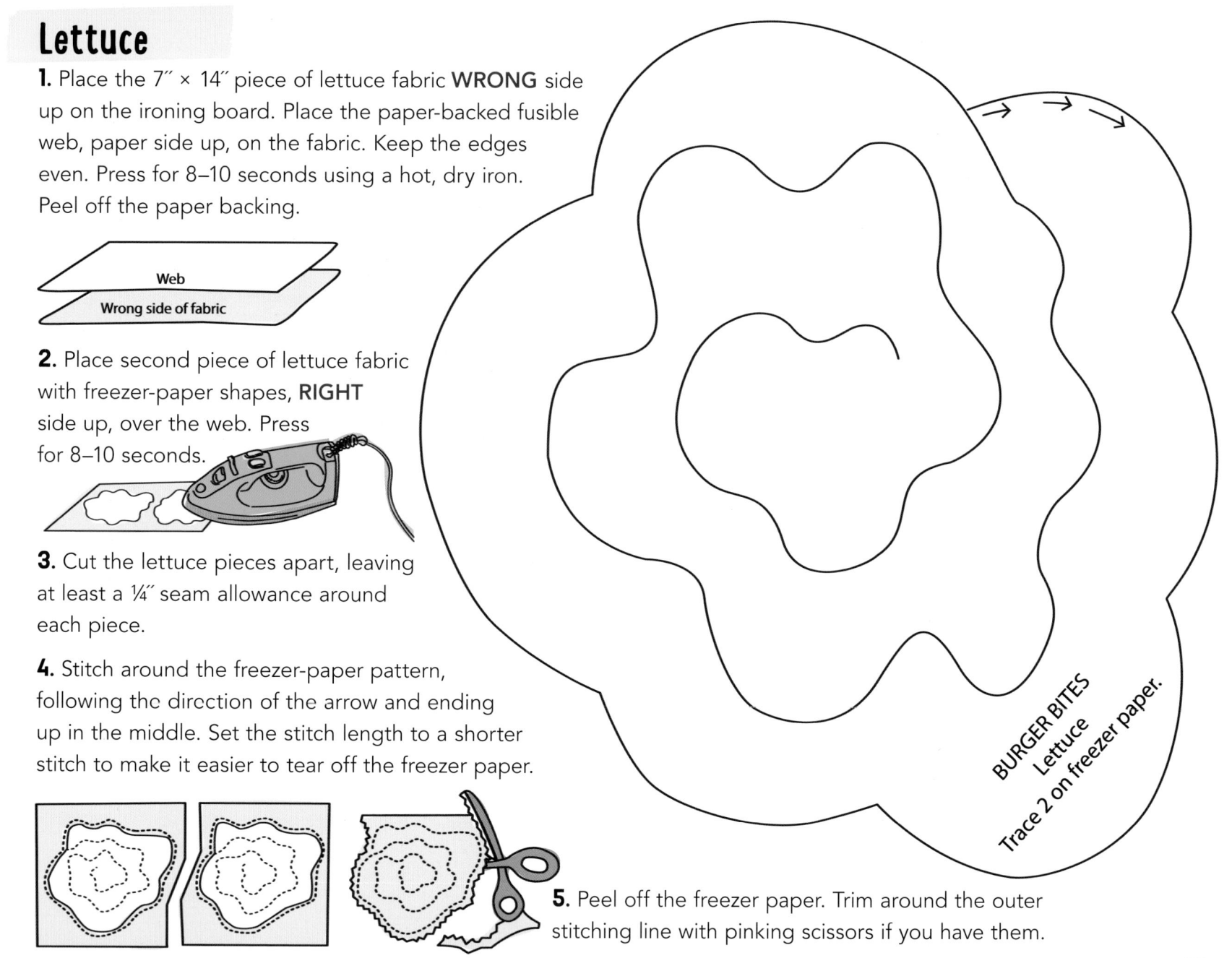

BURGER BITES
Lettuce
Trace 2 on freezer paper.

Tomato and Onion

1. LAYER IN ORDER:

A. 1 square of batting

B. Tomato fabric, **RIGHT** side up

C. Tomato fabric with freezer-paper pattern, **WRONG** side up

2. LAYER IN ORDER:

A. 1 square of batting

B. Onion fabric, **RIGHT** side up

C. Onion fabric with freezer-paper pattern, **WRONG** side up

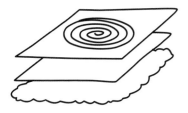

3. Stitch around the circles, leaving an opening to turn.

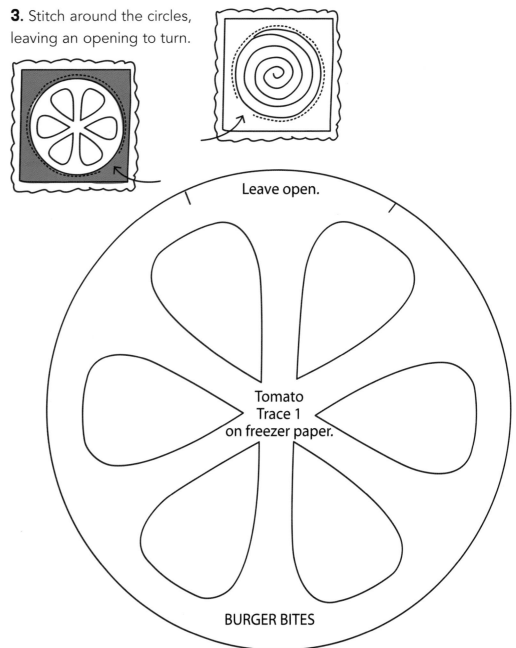

Leave open.

Tomato
Trace 1
on freezer paper.

BURGER BITES

4. Peel off and save the freezer-paper circles. Trim ¼˝ beyond the stitched line.

5. Turn the circles right side out. Push out the seam allowances until smooth. Whipstitch the opening closed with matching thread.

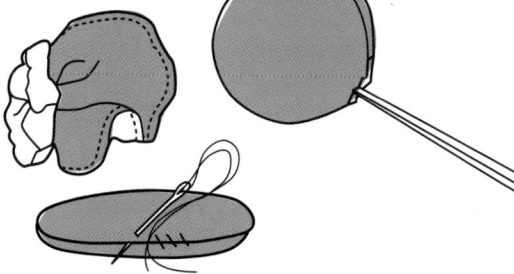

6. Press the freezer paper back onto the onion and tomato pieces. Set the stitch length to a shorter stitch to make it easier to tear off the freezer paper.

7. Stitch the interior lines of the tomato with yellow thread. Stitch the interior lines of the onion with purple thread. Peel off the freezer paper.

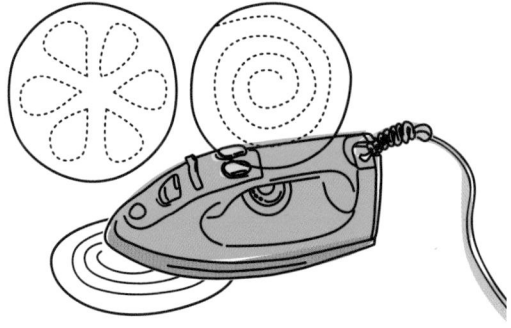

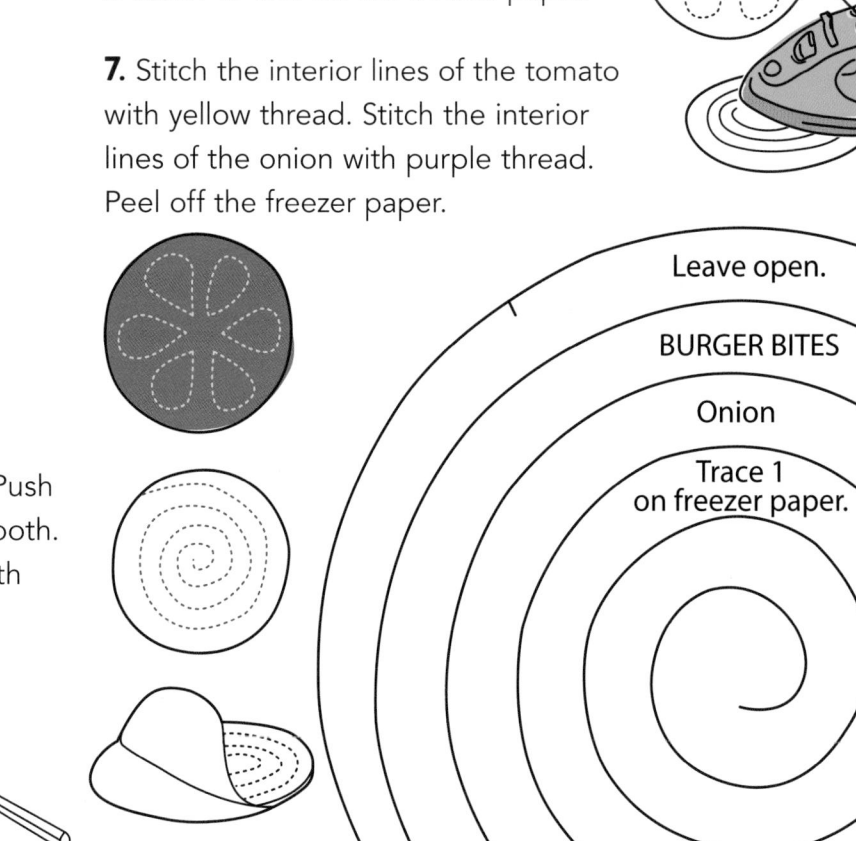

Leave open.

BURGER BITES

Onion

Trace 1 on freezer paper.

Cheese

1. LAYER IN ORDER:

A. Fabric, **WRONG** side up

B. 1 square of batting

C. Fabric with freezer-paper pattern, **RIGHT** side up

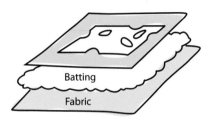

Batting

Fabric

2. Stitch around all the cut edges of the freezer paper. Peel off the freezer paper.

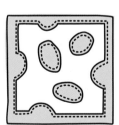

Remember This Point!

To begin cutting the inside of a shape, fold it in half and clip the fold. Then continue cutting through the hole.

3. Trim the cheese ¼″ beyond the stitching lines, and cut out the holes.

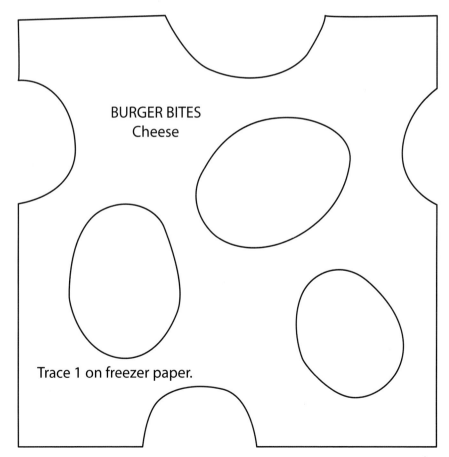

BURGER BITES
Cheese

Trace 1 on freezer paper.

TREASURE POUCH

Here's a pouch with lots of pockets to hold your earbuds, electronic chargers, and secret treasures!

READY?

cotton fabric:

- ☐ 13″ × 26″ rectangle for outside (large circle)

- ☐ 10″ × 19″ rectangle for inside (medium circle)

- ☐ ¼″-wide ribbon: 2½ yards (2.3 m)

- ☐ copy paper

- ☐ paper clips

- ☐ masking tape

- ☐ small safety pin

- ☐ matching thread

- ☐ sewing basket (page 23)

- ☐ freezer paper (see Helper Star Hint, page 33) cut into 3 squares:

  - 1 square 13″ × 13″ (33 cm × 33 cm) (LARGE)

  - 1 square 10″ × 10″ (26 cm × 26 cm) (MEDIUM)

  - 1 square 5″ × 5″ (13 cm × 13 cm) (SMALL)

SET?

1. Trace the 2 circle wedges and the small half-circle on copy paper. To download and print the patterns, refer to About This Book (page 5). Mark the lines on the small circle as dark as possible. Cut them out.

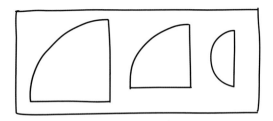

2. Fold the large and medium freezer-paper squares into quarters. Fold the small square in half.

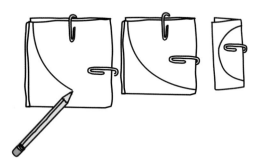

3. Place the patterns on the freezer paper. Match the straight edges with the fold lines. Hold them in place with a paper clip. Trace the curved edges.

4. Leave the squares paper-clipped together and cut along the curved lines. Unfold and you should have 3 nice, even circles.

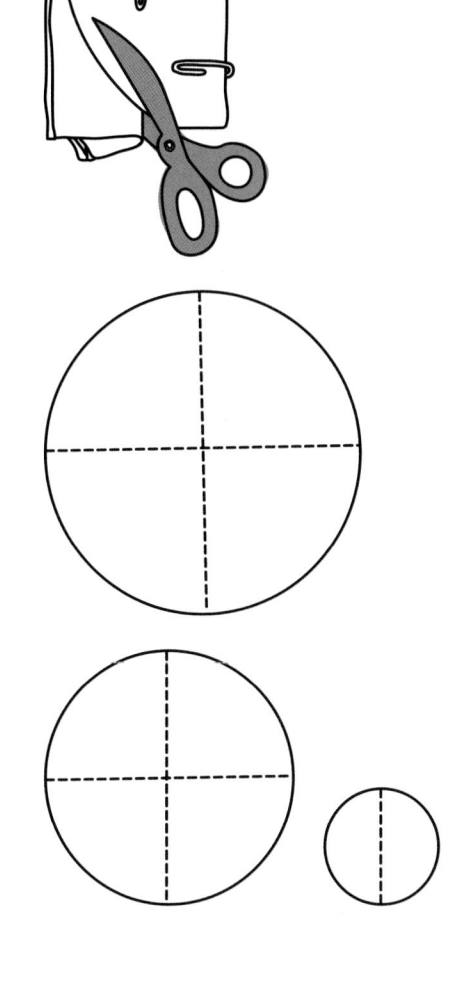

5. Trace the straight lines on the dull side of the small circle, marking them all the way across for later use as a stitching guide. Set the circle aside.

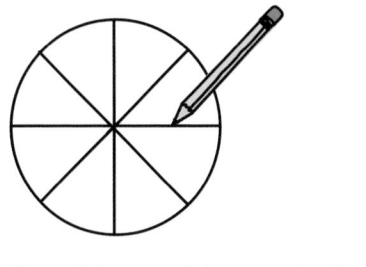

6. Fold your fabric in half with the **RIGHT** sides together.

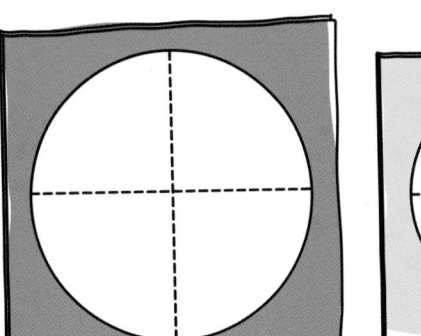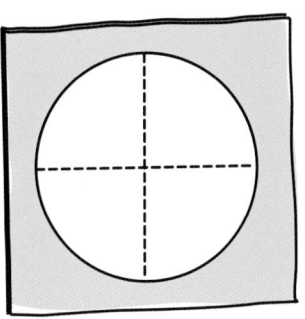

7. Place the large and medium freezer-paper circles on each fabric, shiny side down. Keep the circles at least ½˝ from the edge of fabric. Set the iron to a cotton setting. Press for 5 seconds. If the circles do not stick, press again. Pin through the fabric and paper layers.

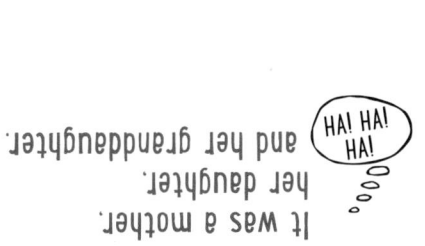

☞ Two mothers and two daughters went to a sewing class.

Each made a Treasure Pouch, but they only made three Treasure Pouches in all.

How is this so?

It was a mother, her daughter, and her granddaughter. *HA! HA! HA!*

118

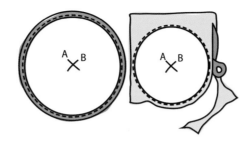

3. Cut the circles out ¼″ away from the stitching line.

6. Insert a dull table knife into the circles through the X's. Push out the edges with the knife, making them smooth. Press the edges, using the knife to get a smooth edge.

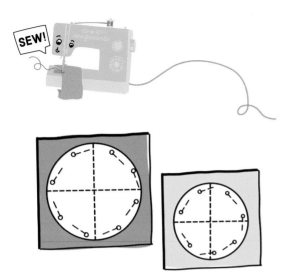

1. Stitch next to the freezer-paper circles. Remove the pins.

2. Mark an X in the centers of the freezer-paper circles.

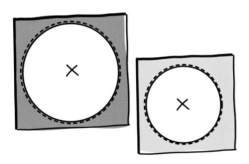

4. Pull the fabric layers apart on each circle. Fold along Line A and snip Line B. Refold along Line B and snip Line A. Be sure not to cut into the bottom circle fabric. Peel off the freezer paper.

5. Turn the circles right side out through the X's. Shake the circles.

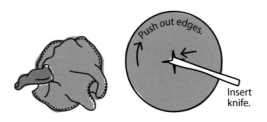

Push out edges.

Insert knife.

Remember This Point!

A casing is 2 rows of parallel stitching that create a tunnel for elastic or ribbon.

7. Make a casing for the ribbon on the large circle.

A. Place a piece of masking tape ½˝ to the right of the needle hole.

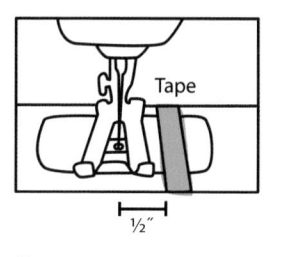

B. Place the circle under the needle with the edge next to the masking tape.

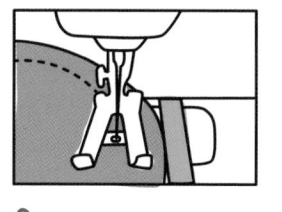

C. Stitch around the circle, back-stitching at the beginning and end.

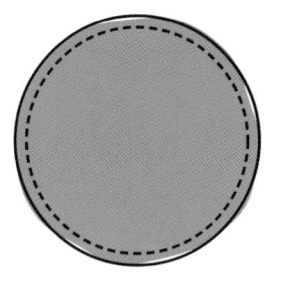

D. Place a second piece of masking tape 1˝ to the right of the needle hole.

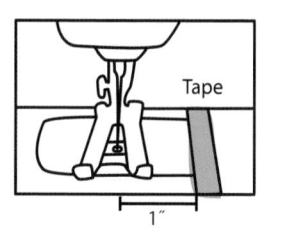

E. Place the circle under the needle with the edge next to the second piece of masking tape.

F. Stitch around the circle as before.

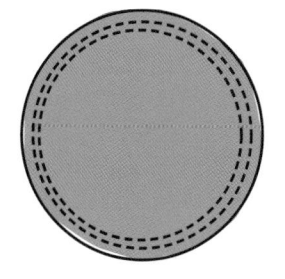

8. Press the large and medium circles into quarters to find the exact center.

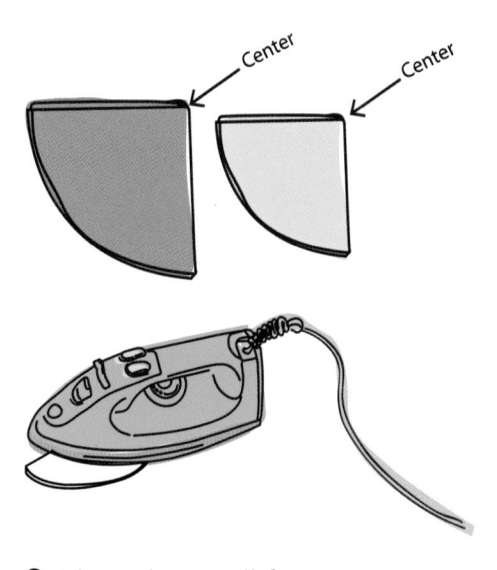

9. Place the small freezer-paper circle on top of the medium circle, on the side without the cut X. Match the centers. Press for 5 seconds.

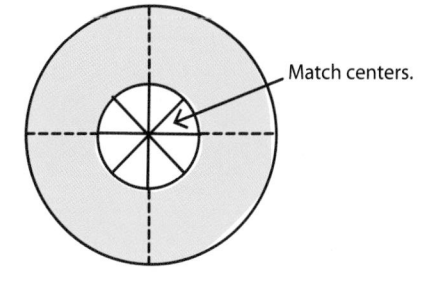

Match centers.

10. With a pencil and a ruler, extend the lines on the freezer paper to the edges of the fabric circle.

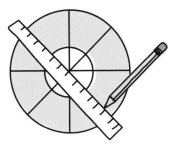

11. Place this circle over the large circle, with the cut X sides together. Match the centers and fold lines. Pin.

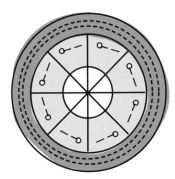

12. Stitch around the small freezer-paper circle. Stitch across all of the lines to the outside edge of the medium circle. Backstitch at each end. This creates the pockets. Peel off the freezer paper.

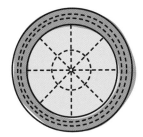

13. On the outside of the large circle, mark and cut 2 small slits between the casing lines directly across from each other. Cut through 1 layer of fabric only. Use small, sharp-pointed scissors or a seam ripper.

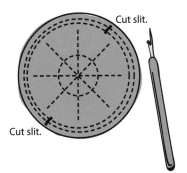

Cut slit.

Cut slit.

14. Cut the ribbon in half. Pin the safety pin to one end of the ribbon. Starting at 1 slit, push the safety pin through the casing all the way around the circle to the same slit. Tie the ribbon ends together. Do not gather the circle—try to keep it flat.

Helper Star Hint

It may be necessary to help the sewist cut the slits. Do not cut through the stitching. If a mistake is made, resew across the casing lines.

15. Pin the safety pin to the second piece of ribbon. Start at the other slit and push the safety pin through the casing all the way around the circle. Keep the circle flat. Remove the safety pin. Tie the ribbon ends together.

16. Pull the ribbons to close the bag. Adjust the gathers. Fill all the pockets.

Tie ends.

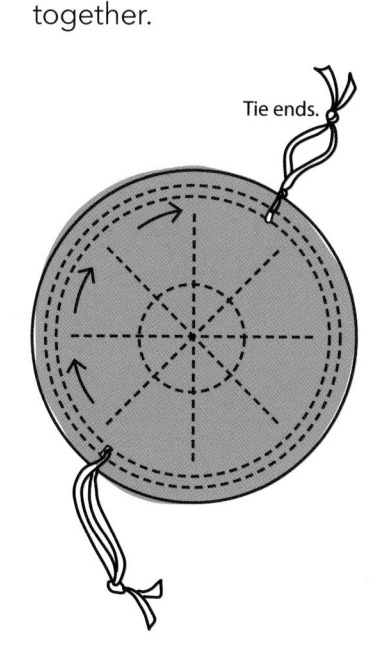

Knock, knock.

Who's there?

Hugh.

Hugh who?

HA! HA! HA!

Hugh tired of knock-knock jokes yet?

122

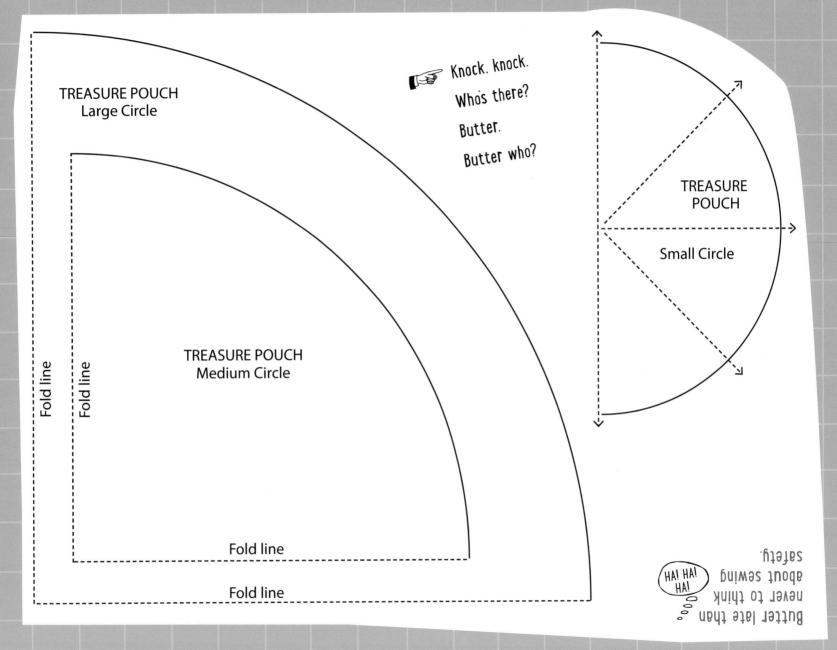

TREASURE POUCH
Large Circle

TREASURE POUCH
Medium Circle

Fold line

Fold line

Fold line

Fold line

Knock. knock.

Who's there?

Butter.

Butter who?

TREASURE
POUCH

Small Circle

Butter late than
never to think
about sewing
safely.

HA! HA!
HA!

PUZZLE ANSWERS

SAFETY FIRST >> on page 7

1. Damaged sewing machine cord

2. Iron not standing upright

3. Finger under the needle

4. Eyes not watching the needle

5. Open scissors about to fall

6. Pins on floor

7. Cord across doorway

8. Food at sewing machine

9. Dog under ironing board

10. Pins held in mouth

PATTI'S PUZZLE >> on page 14

STITCH ALONG >> on page 17

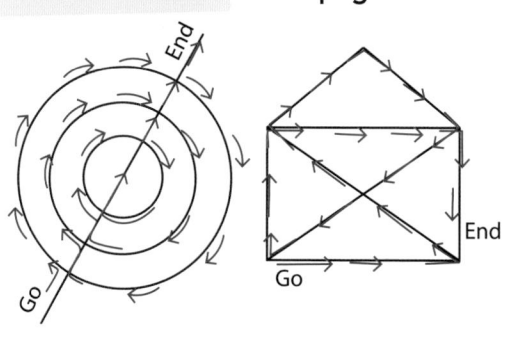

TANGLED THREADS >> on page 18

serveer reevl ro nottub	reverse lever or button
sseerrp toof	presser foot
thicst gelnth sorteecl	stitch length selector
bibbon	bobbin
helewylf	flywheel
no/fof chwits	on/off switch
cishtt thwid loreects	stitch width selector
loosp nip	spool pin
defe odsg	feed dogs
rohtta tepla	throat plate
nestnio troncol	tension control
leeend	needle
dareth degiu	thread guide
otof dalep	foot pedal
dareth kate-pu	thread take-up
nobbib drwine	bobbin winder
serpers ooft terfil	presser foot lifter
gitlh	light

```
M  F  L  Y  W  H  E  E  L  G
W  E  S  T  P  K  P  W  S  Y
D  E  Q  X  I  Z  J  B  K  E
V  D  T  E  N  S  I  O  N  L
P  D  H  H  S  T  C  B  M  D
I  O  G  P  R  I  G  B  K  E
R  G  I  L  N  T  V  I  C  E
Q  S  L  U  B  C  F  N  D  N
H  M  T  G  L  H  J  W  X  W
S  R  O  S  S  I  C  S  T  Q
```

as	came	sane
awe	mane	swam
awes	manes	sham
aim	main	ham
aims	name	hams
can	names	shame
cane	same	shaming
canes	wane	man
cam	wanes	ma

magic	nags	seen	hem	mica	shin
hang	hag	sheen	hems	mice	sic
hangs	hags	gene	hen	wise	sing
sang	game	semi	hens	win	singe
was	games	he	hew	wine	siege
saw	mange	hence	hews	wins	sigh
has	manse	she	mew	his	sign
wan	manic	when	mews	shine	sigma
waning	machine	new	mewing	swine	wing
maw	ace	news	men	swing	wings
maws	aces	chew	mean	swim	since
sag	mace	seem	means	whine	inch
shag	case	seeming	meaning	whines	inches
sage	cases	sea	meanings	chime	wish
snag	ache	seam	is	chimes	wishing
wag	aches	seaming	in	niche	him
wags	aching	séance	image	niches	wig
wage	sac	scheme	sin	hinge	wigs
wages	each	wean	sine	mine	whim
gas	ease	weans	since	mini	shim
ash	ewe	weaning	sinew	nine	whims
cash	ewes	sew	wince	nines	winch
mash	me	sewing	winces	gin	winches
caw	we	sewn	whence	chin	winching
caws	wee	gem	wench	chins	
nag	see	gems	mince	china	

BUILDING BLOCKS >> on page 22

1. presser foot lifter
2. stitch length selector
3. stitch width selector
4. flywheel
5. tension control
6. feed dogs
7. on/off switch
8. reverse lever or button
9. thread guide
10. bobbin
11. foot pedal
12. light
13. bobbin winder
14. throat plate
15. spool pin
16. presser foot
17. thread take-up
18. needle

SEWING BASKET >> on page 23

☐ scissors for cutting paper
☐ scissors for cutting fabric
☐ pinking scissors
☐ sewing machine needles
☐ hand-sewing needles
☐ pins
☐ pincushion
☐ thread
☐ pencil
☐ ruler
☐ tape measure
☐ seam ripper
☐ iron
☐ ironing board
☐ wastebasket

CROSSWORD PUZZLE >> on page 28

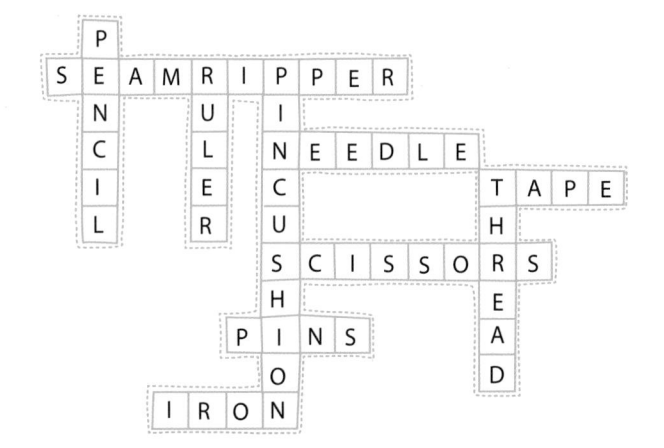

DRIVER'S TRAINING >> on page 30

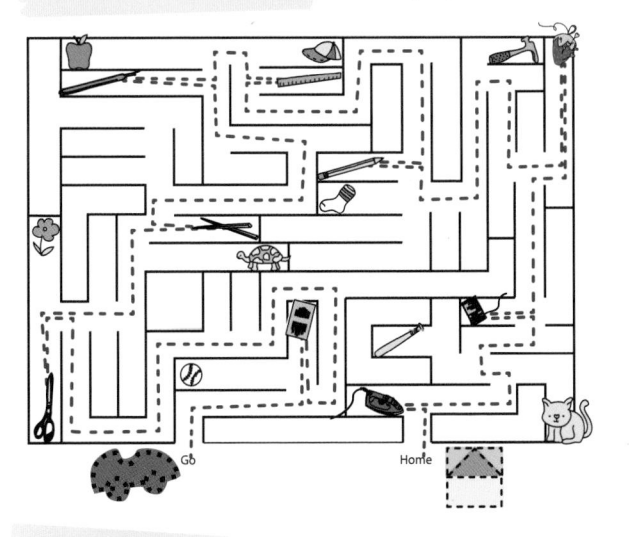

MEASURE UP >> on page 51

D, G, C, A, F, B, E

CRAZY CORDS >> on page 69

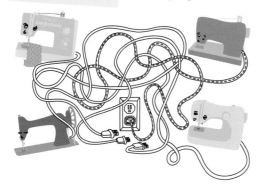

SUPER SEWIST'S SECRET CODE 1
>> on page 75

Super sewists sew straight seams.

FRED'S THREAD >> on page 85

SECRET CODE 2 >> on page 91

Stitching is stupendous.

UP WITH LETTERS >> on page 92

1. bobbin

2. tape measure

3. throat plate

4. thread

5. scissors

6. press

7. buttons

8. pins

9. flywheel

10. foot pedal

11. pivot

12. needle

SECRET CODE 3 >> on page 97

Patti practices perfect pivots.

SEWING SILLIES >> on page 98

1. spool pin

2. flywheel

3. feed dogs

4. throat plate

5. pincushion

6. tape measure

7. dust bunny

8. freezer paper

DON'T LET UP >> on page 99

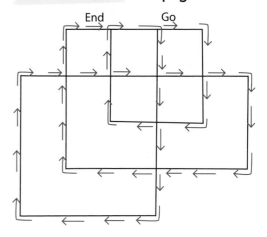

WORD SEARCH 2 >> on page 105

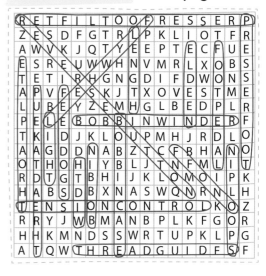

FunStitch
STUDIO

> "Every time I finish a project, **I get so excited**, because I feel like I can do **anything!**"
> —Annalise, age 12

FunStitch Studio books are written and designed specifically with kids, tweens, and teens in mind!

The text and projects are age appropriate and *nurture the love of handmade* in budding sewists, quilters, embroiderers, and fashion designers.

See the complete list of FunStitch Studio titles at ctpub.com/funstitch-studio

by Lenka Vodicka-Paredes and Asia Currie

by Maryellen Kim

by Lynn Koolish, Kerry Graham, and Mary Wruck

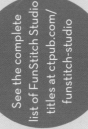

by Sophie Kerr with Weeks Ringle and Bill Kerr

FunStitch STUDIO   an imprint of C&T Publishing